Spending Your Way To The Poorhouse

by

Tommy L. Gardner

ISBN: 1-4140-5556-0 (e-book)
ISBN: 1-4140-5555-2 (Paperback)

Printed in the United States of America
Bloomington, IN

This book is printed on acid free paper.

1stBooks - rev. 01/16/04

INTRODUCTION

Many of you will ask yourself if you know what a poorhouse is. Most will either know what it is or will be curious enough to read on and see if you're right. Others will think I've invaded their privacy.

The last few pages will discuss poorhouses of the past, how they were operated and who dwelled there. The remainder of the book will hopefully help you understand how you got into financial trouble and what you can do to climb out of it and rescue yourself. My hope is that you'll keep an open mind and find a way to a more secure future.

Getting around in the financial turmoil that surrounds us today takes a lot of planning, dedication and desire to take control of our lives. When I was a boy, things were more simple. Today, we're deluged with every reason to buy, buy and buy. The only way out is it decide you can overcome these temptations and get you and yours on the road to a more successful and enjoyable future.

My wife, Cherrie, has been with me for almost thirty years. She's put up with my frugal lifestyle and my ways of dealing with financial problems. I've had my share, and so will you.

This book is presented in very short chapters of various scenarios of spending, saving, and how to do both. I honestly hope you can get something from the book that will help you get into better financial shape and stay that way.

Many of you are already in the poorhouse. It's not a big white house up on the hill, but your current situation, over which you must regain control. My hope is that you will find things within this book that will improve your financial life.

Table of Contents

WHAT IS MONEY?

Could you give a good example if asked what you think money is? It's a strange thing. We want it. We need it. We depend on it. We try to make it grow. It can't change shape or size to grow. We must have more of it to make it grow. But, what is it, really? Money is a tool to use to exchange for goods or services that satisfy our needs and wants. Without money, our lives would be very difficult. We accept money from our employer in exchange for work performed. It's what the cashier accepts in exchange for bread, milk, clothing, etc.

Ask yourself these questions. Do I want to keep track of my spending and savings? Do I want to make better spending decisions? How much money do I really receive? How much can I afford to save, and how much do I want to save? Am I willing to risk my money to try to gain more? Am I willing to sacrifice today to have more money in the future?

It can be said that money is a medium of exchange. Two or more persons agree on the use of the money and are willing to trade their resources for money, understanding that they can trade the money for something they want. They exchange the money for goods and goods for money.

Any two people may want things of different values. Money is a standard of value. How many shirts is a pair of shoes worth? Prices allow us to compare the values of our resources and the things we just have to have. Do you think a dollar is 100 cents, 10 dimes or 20 nickels? They're all the same.

Money retains its value over time, for the most part. You can sell or trade for money one day and buy something at a later date. It is still worth what you thought when you received it.

There are many different kinds of money. The ones we recognize are paper currency and coins. We use dollar bills, nickels, pennies, dimes, quarters, etc. every day. The U.S. mints produce coins and paper money for us to use for exchange. Money cannot be absolutely guaranteed by the government. Our currency was once backed by the govern-ment and could be traded for gold or silver. If anyone doubted the value of money, they could trade it for gold or silver. Today, there is not enough gold and silver to trade for all the money. We have decided that we have faith in the value of money, so we don't need the gold standard. Much of the world seems to have faith in our money's value. The dollar is the common medium for exchange around the world.

Most individual transactions may be made with cash. Most of our large purchases and those that do not require immediate cash payment are made with other forms of money. Believe it or not, a check is considered money. Checking account balances make up a majority of the total supply of money. A check is simply a note to the bank asking the bank to give some of the money in your account to another person or business. If the

Person you're buying from believes you really do have enough funds in your account, they'll take a check and deposit it into their account.

Considering checking account fees, which type account is right for you? If you write just a few checks a month, you may have to pay a few cents for each check unless your balance is up to a certain level. If you write a lot of checks, a flat fee may be better. Why pay for other bank services if you don't plan to use them?

If you find yourself having to use an ATM machine because you didn't write a check for enough money to cover the day's expenses, it'll cost you extra money. They are costly ways of accessing your money. Some banks charge fees to use their cards in an ATM machine. Sometimes, the owner of the ATM will charge a fee if you don't have an account with their bank. It is possible that both banks will charge your account a fee. Even if you use a "no fee" machine, your bank will charge you a fee. Remember these charges when you balance your bankbook.

A relatively new item is the debit card. Using it causes a transaction that auto-matically reduces your bank account by the amount spent. With a credit card, you have a grace period, a time within which you can pay the balance without additional cost. Debit cards are similar to writing a check. Many merchants limit the amount of debit card transaction. You can't buy things like appliances with a debit card. Banks also issue check cards that are processed just like a check.

If your credit has gotten to the point that people require a money order instead of a check, you are in serious trouble. And you'll have to purchase the money order before you put an amount on it, costing you another dollar or more.

If you're in a good situation that lets you actually save some money, ask yourself these few questions. How assessable do I want my money to be? How much interest will I earn? Is there any possibility that I will lose my money?

If saving for a short time or for an emergency, you want an account that has easy access to your money, such as a passbook savings account or a money market account. Even a checking account is okay. If you're saving for years ahead, it is better to save so you won't be tempted to get to the money as quickly.

If a higher interest rate is what you want, choose a cd. The money remains in the account for a specific period of time. The longer the time, the higher the rate. You may want to invest in a cd for a period of time to finally use it and interest it earned to pay off that car loan financed at a higher rate of interest. This is saving money, using low-earning money to pay off higher interest loans.

Savings accounts pay a fixed rate of interest. Investment accounts may gain or lose. A blend of savings and investment accounts may work well for you. The key is deciding why you are saving and how much you can afford to save.

Save for a short-term for a night out by dropping a little change into a jar each day. Long-term goals such as a home purchase or college require putting money into a place where it will grow. If you are saving for a car, etc., keep the money in a place where you won't be tempted to spend it. For your retirement, you want to save in a safe way and in a way that gives you the best long-term return for your deposits.

Save early. When interest compounds, interest is paid on interest. Joe puts $1,000 in a savings account at 5 % interest. After one year, the account balance was $1,50. A total of $50 is paid to Joe's account. After another year, his balance was $1,102.50. The interest was $50 on the original $1,000 and another $2.50 interest on the $50 interest from the first year. Another x interest rate amount + interest earned adds up. Try it.

CAN MONEY BUY HAPPINESS?

Can money buy happiness? Well, yes and no. Yes, in that money can buy things like food, shelter, clothing, etc. These things are essential for happiness unless you're satisfied to go nude, go hungry and live in a cave. People who do not have money to buy these basic essentials will, most likely, be less happy than someone who does. Someone who has a lot of money is not necessarily happier than someone who just has the basics. Surveys show rich people are no happier than those with modest incomes.

Of course, money can give you more freedom and the control to do what they want to do. The rich also need meaningful activities. If you have a lot of money and no mean-ingful endeavors other than gaining material goods, you'll feel unfulfilled.

Some people will spend so much time trying to obtain wealth that they don't find those things that will bring them happiness, like time with the family and other enjoyable activities.

You may save some money with the following tips. It pays to shop around. Phone stores instead of driving there in person to inquire about products. It will save time and gasoline. Try to avoid impulse buying. Ask yourself if you really need that item. Try to eat out at restaurants as little as possible. Use those coupons. Buy things that are on sale. Subscribe to Consumer Reports Magazine to get information about the item or service you're looking for, learn unbiased evaluations to help you get a reliable product that will Be enjoyed. Ask about potential discounts. It won't hurt. Do it yourself. Mow your own lawn, and wash your own car. Just think of all the money you'll save, and the exercise won't hurt.

You can lower the airline ticket as much as two thirds by making certain

4

the trip includes a Saturday evening stay-over, and by buying the ticket well in advance. Call all airlines that fly where you want to go and ask what the lowest fare is to your destination. Compare prices on the Internet. Keep an eye out for "fare wars." Be prepared to act quickly.

When renting a car, shop around for the best basic rate and special offers. Rental companies offer insurance and waiver options. Check with your insurance agent to avoid duplicating coverage.

When buying that new car, you can save thousands of dollars over the lifetime of the car by selecting a reliable car that is not bad on repairs. See Consumer Reports Magazine for important comparisons. You can save hundreds by comparison shopping. Use the Internet to find out what the invoice price is. Call several dealers for price quotes, and let each know you are calling the others. Don't discuss a trade-in until the deal is made on the price.

Before buying a used car, compare the seller's asking price with the average retail price in a "bluebook" or other guides at libraries, banks and credit unions. Have a mechanic you trust look the car over good. Consider purchasing a used car from an individual you know and trust. They are more likely to charge a lower price and let you know the truth about the car's condition.

Don't lease a car just because the payments are lower. They're lower because you don't own the car at the end of the lease. Leases are complicated. When shopping, consider the price of the car, your trade-in allowance, down payment, monthly payments, certain fees for things like excess mileage, excess wear and tear and the cost of buying the car at the end of the lease.

You can save hundreds of dollars a year by pumping gasoline yourself and using the lowest octane rating shown in your owner's manual. Keep the engine tuned and tires at the right inflation pressure. When buying a car, buy a fuel efficient one.

When considering car repairs, consumers lose billions of dollars annually on unneeded and poorly done repairs. Find a skilled, honest mechanic. Look for a mechanic who is certified and well established in the area, has done good work for someone you know and who communicates repair options and associated costs.

When purchasing car insurance, you can save lots of money by purchasing it from a licensed, low-price insurer. Call your state insurance commissioner office for a listing showing prices charged by different companies. Call several of the lowest priced, licensed insurers to learn charges for the same coverage. Talk to the agent about raising your deductibles on collision and comprehensive coverage to at least $500. Make sure the new policy is in effect before dropping the old one.

With homeowners insurance, you can save by purchasing insurance from a low price, licensed insurer. Your state insurance commissioner office can show you charges from various companies. Make sure you purchase enough coverage to replace the house and the contents. Get replacement value on the contents.

When buying life insurance, buy term life insurance. If buying whole life insurance, plan to hold it for at least 15 years. You'll double your insurance costs by canceling policies after only a few years.

With a checking account, you can save by selecting an account with a minimum balance requirement that you can handle. Banks will often drop or lower checking fees if paychecks are to be directly deposited by your employer. Direct deposit offers security, convenience and access immediately to your money.

Before opening a savings or investment account with a bank, find out if the account is insured by the federal government. Sometimes, mutual funds and annuities are not. Consider CD's or treasury bills to get the maximum yield %

With credit cards, try to pay off the balance monthly when due. If you can't do this, switch to a card with a lower annual percentage rate. You can get a listing of these rates from Bankcard Holders of America for a modest fee by calling 703-389-5445. You can reduce fees by getting rid of all but one or two cards, by avoiding late payment fees, etc.

When looking for an auto loan, try to make a large down payment or even paying for it in cash. Finance charges are very large if you don't. Shop for the cheapest loan. Contact several banks, a credit union or finance with the carmaker's own finance company.

Looking for the right mortgage loan is very important. On a $100,000 fixed rate loan at 8% APR, you will pay $90,000 less in interest on a 15 year loan than on a 30 year loan. Also, shop for the lowest points. On a 15 year $100,000 fixed rate mortgage, lowering the APR from 8.5% to 8.0% saves more than $5,000 in interest charges. On this mortgage, paying two points instead of three will save another $1,000. Call several lenders for information about rates, points and fees. Interest rates on adjustable rate mortgage loans can vary a lot over the lifetime of the mortgage. An increase of several percentage points may raise payments by hundreds of dollars a month.

When refinancing a mortgage, consider that you should get a rate that is at least one percentage point lower than your existing rate and plan to keep the new mortgage for several years or more.

Be cautious in taking out home equity loans. This type of loan reduces your equity you've built in your home. You could lose your home if unable to make the payments. Compare home equity loans offered by at least four banking institutions. Consider not only the annual percentage rate, but also the points, closing costs, other fees, and the index for any variable rate changes.

When purchasing a home, you can often negotiate a lower sale price by employing a buyer broker who works for you, not the seller. Do not purchase any house until it has been examined by a home inspector you have selected.

If you rent a place to live, do not limit your rental search to classified ads or referrals from your friends. Select buildings where you would like to live and contact the building manager or owner to see if anything is available. Remember, signing a lease obligates you to make all monthly payments for the term of the agreement.

Home repairs often cost thousands of dollars and are subject to complaints. Select from a well-established, licensed contractor who has submitted written, fixed price bids for the work. Do not sign a contract that requires full payment before the work has been completed to your satisfaction.

Consult Consumer Reports for information about certain brands and how to evaluate them, including energy use. Price and quality differences vary vastly among brands. After you've selected a brand, find several stores which carry that brand. Phone them for quotes, asking for the lowest price they can offer you. This comparison shopping may save you $100 or more.

To save hundreds of dollars annually on electricity, make sure that any new appliance you purchase, especially air conditioners and furnaces, are energy-efficient. Information on the efficiency ratings is found on Energy Guide Labels required by federal law. You may enroll in a load management program or other programs offered by your electric utility to save money on the cost of electricity.

You may save hundreds of dollars a year on home heating by getting a home energy audit. Your electric or gas utility company may do this audit for free or for a small fee.

Check with your phone company to see if a flat rate or measured service plan will save the most money. You will usually save money by buying instead of leasing your phone. Check your local phone bill to see if you have optional services that you don't need. Each option you drop may save you $40 or more a year.

For entertainment, read an online newspaper instead of subscribing to one. Both money and trees will be saved. Most newspapers have online versions. Inexpensive internet access to certain sites may cost you a few dollars a month. Check out a book from the library instead of buying it at a bookstore. Go to a park for quiet time. Go for a walk or maybe a bike ride.

When shopping for groceries, you can save money shopping at lower priced food stores. Those convenience stores charge much more. Shop from a list and stick to it. Compare prices per ounce or other units of measure.

Can money buy happiness? Sure it can. It can also cause you more misery than you can imagine. Use it correctly, and it will make your life much easier and happier.

IT'S EASY! WE'LL JUST FINANCE IT ON THE CARD.

Most people think the only things financed are cars, homes, boats, etc. The truth is that if you don't pay the balance of your credit card(s) at the end of the month, you're financing things you wouldn't think of doing otherwise. Can you imagine going to the bank and asking for a loan to buy groceries, gas for the car, clothing for the kids, tickets to a wrestling match or even a casual meal out. When you let the balance go over and pay finance charges, you're adding all the stuff you bought and paid for to your present items you have financed.

If you pay $1.30 a gallon for gas and don't pay the balance at month end, you could be financing that gas for years and end up paying $4.00 or so a gallon for it. That's absurd, isn't it? You could pay $300 for a pair of shoes, $200 for a meal, or even $600 for a $70 motel bill for a night.

The credit card has taken the place of going to the bank, sitting in front of a loan officer and embarrassing yourself asking for money. With the card, you simply obtain cash at a local ATM machine or just hand it to the clerk when you make a purchase. It's almost painless at the time. The pain comes when the bill comes due and you can't afford to pay the balance. And the interest rate could be as much as 28% instead of 10% at a bank. I'm not saying to finance such at a bank. There's a simple rule for the use of a credit card. If you don't have money in your checking account to buy it without the card, don't buy it.

Making minimum payments on a card balance of a few thousand dollars will require paying for that stuff long after the car, and maybe the home is paid for.

When I was twenty-one, I charged a washer and dryer at a large chain store. They cost only $360 total. I paid about $30 a month for about 30 months and still owed a large balance. I went to a local bank and borrowed money to pay off the debt. The banker told me I couldn't borrow my way out of debt. I said I could this time, but never again. Since then, I have never let a card balance go unpaid fully at month end.

My wife, Cherrie, and I were checking out of a Florida motel. A couple younger than us attempted to use a credit card to pay room charges. They were told that they couldn't use that card, that it was full. After trying several cards and being told the same thing time after time, the young man told the clerk he'd just have to pay cash for the bill. I thought we had to pay for everything, not pretend that using a credit card wasn't the same thing as paying cash for it.

Combining card balances only prolongs the eventual demise of your finances. Some even mortgage the house to pay off credit card balances. Don't ever do this.

Wean yourself off the cards. Use only one card for gas for the vehicle. Then pay the balance when due. You've then used their money a month interest free instead of financing what you bought.

HOW MUCH IS ENOUGH

How much money is enough? How big does your car have to be? How many rooms does your house have to have? Maybe you've never asked yourself these questions. Maybe you should.

I've known people who had vast amounts of money, stocks, etc. who never thought they had enough. Why? It's because they knew they could obtain more. How did they get all that wealth? It had to come from someone in the form of hard work, luck or good investing, criminal activities, etc. Most comes from long periods of hard work and the desire to achieve a goal. When you accumulate wealth, some loses theirs. They must then get theirs from someone else. Are you a loser or a winner? It's possible for every-body to be a winner.

I remember a joke about an old farmer who had a mule. He sold it to his neighbor for $20. Later, he bought it back for $30, then sold it back to the neighbor for $40. This went on for years. One day the farmer went over to buy back the mule. His neighbor told him that he had sold the mule to somebody else. The other farmer said that was crazy, that they were both getting rich with that mule.

Don't get me wrong. There's nothing wrong with having a little money ahead. The fact is that a very small percent of us have any extra money at all. Why? It's probably not because we haven't earned a lot of money. It's probably because we spend all or more than we earn. I told my son two ways to stay ahead. One is to earn more than you spend. The other is to spend less than you earn. They sound like the same thing, right? Actually, the amount you earn has far less to do with it than the amount you spend. Live within your means.

Ask ten people how much they make. About eight of them won't have any idea. Most will tell you how much they bring home. Ask people who get a tax

11

refund how much they pay in taxes. They'll tell you they don't pay taxes, that they get a refund. This is the way most people think. You've paid federal tax, state tax, all sort of insurances and other amounts before you see your paycheck. Now the trick is to know how to hold onto some of what is left. That's where most money problems begin.

Look in your closet. How many dollars worth of clothing do you see? You'll under-state it. Add them up and you'll be amazed. Then think of what percent of the time you wear some of them.

Look at your vehicle. How many will it seat? Do you need seating for eight when you drive alone or with one or two others most of the time? How much is enough? Your cost of insurance, taxes, etc. are in direct proportion to make and size of your vehicle. If you're taking a trip and need seating for eight, simply rent a van. Even rent for a week is less than a monthly car payment, and it's over in a week, not 60 months.

When you gas up that fuel-guzzler, what octane fuel do you pump? Look at your owner's manual to see the required octane. You could be paying $.10 to $.20 too much per gallon. That's about $160 a year, enough to pay for the tag tax for a year or more.

Think of how much is enough, not how much you want. If you don't have six kids or run a day care pick-up service, why do you need the three rows of seats in the small bus you drive?

IT'S NOT HARD TO MEET EXPENSES. THEY'RE EVERYWHERE.

Have you ever heard someone say they couldn't meet expenses? Expenses are everywhere. The amount you meet depends on how many you create. They're like your kids. You created them. You're obligated to take care of them. Like having children, just simply stop creating them, and someday you can see the light at the end of the tunnel.

If you had notes hanging from strings from the ceiling of your living room and had to walk through them every day, you'd get a better insight into the enormity of bills you've created. You have the ability to create or not create such bills. I know utility bills, groceries, car maintenance, taxes and insurance have to be paid by everyone. I'm talking about credit card bills, clothing bills, boating expenses, four-wheeler associated costs, etc.

If you had to pay all your bills on a daily basis, could you do it? If not, you can't pay them weekly or monthly. If your total monthly bills amount to $2000, you'd owe $92.05 a day. Do you bring home that much? You'd have to make about $146 a day to take that much home after deductions. Remember, most work only five days a week. You have to calculate your bills on the same basis. If you owe $2000 monthly and bring home less than $460 weekly, you can't possibly pay all your bills. You've got to figure out what you can do without or get an extra job.

Do you spend more on weekends than on weekdays? Almost all people do because they're out there running themselves nuts to see what they want to buy or do next. If I spend every weekday in Home Depot, I'd be fatally tempted to buy things I don't need or didn't know how to use.

When you make that walk to the mailbox and discover bills, you don't think you owed them the day before, only now, today. Bills are owed from every dollar you earn, not from the last paycheck of the money. Get used to depositing bill money every week, and you'll discover you probably have a little left over. When a bill is paid off, don't create another one. Keep depositing money for the old bill even though you don't owe it now.

Try this. If you think you can't afford a car payment, simply create one to your savings account. If you can't do this, you can't afford the car.

Try making an effort every time you walk through your living room and run into all those bills hanging down, to pay one of them off as soon as possible. Soon, you won't be running into the bills, and your path will be a little easier to navigate.

I've heard people say they didn't owe anything. They say they have their home and car paid for. I want to ask them why they're still working. If most of your bills are other than for the monthly utilities, insurance, taxes, etc., you're in serious trouble.

So the next time you can't meet expenses, get rid of them one by one, and you can meet those left much more easily.

I DON'T KNOW WHAT WE OWE. SHE PAYS THE BILLS.

Do you know the total of the weekly, monthly, quarterly or yearly bills you owe? Money doesn't go out at the same level it comes in. Some bills are paid yearly, like taxes. Who has the responsibility in your household to be sure the bills are paid? Most of the time, the wife has this unenviable task. If you honestly don't know how much your bills amount to, you have a serious problem.

If you don't know for sure that your bills amount to less than your take-home pay, you have work to do. Some bills can be reduced, some can't. You have control over gas, phone, power and grocery bills. You can chip away at them a little at a time. Other bills for house, car and credit card payments are set, and you cannot reduce them after creating them unless you lose your brain and refinance your home to help pay for them. All you have done then is to guarantee that you'll now owe for a longer period of time.

Husbands and wives should send the kids out to play, turn off the television and sit to go over the bills. Information in prior chapters of this book should help with this un-desirable task. You both may be shocked at the total. You owe them, and both of you are responsible for paying them since both of you created them.

When my son was younger, he had no idea if bills were being paid, only that they weren't doing well financially. One good fatherly talk straightened this out. Now, he actually participates in the paying of the bills.

You should go to the store, buy a ledger book, write the date, to whom, check amount, bank balance, etc. for each transaction. Then, you can often look at what is spent and blame each other for it. My wife and I have kept such records for almost thirty years. I can tell you any check written and the bank balance for any period of time.

Have you heard the statement, "My job is to make the money. Her job is to pay the bills"? Remember, you both make bills. If both are writing checks without knowing if money is left in your account, to cover them you'll go broke quicker than a pine tree in a hurricane. Remember, bills are like children. You both created them. You both are responsible for them. Remember, too, that bills and children can be limited.

If you pay house insurance and property taxes once annually, don't swell with pride if you have a bank balance. You'll soon owe these bills. So, know what and when you owe. Be responsible. Work together to reduce your total bills. Try to save a little, too.

BUT IT ISN'T DUE UNTIL THE END OF THE MONTH.

When do you really have to pay the car payment? It's true it is due once a month, usually at the end of the month. But if you owe a $400 payment, that's $4800 a year. It's also $13.15 a day. You bought the car to drive every day, didn't you?

If your payment is $400 monthly, try this. Every day, even on week-ends, put the $13.15 in a box. Most of you will say you don't think you can do this. If you can't, you can't afford the car. You can't wait until the week the payment is due to come up with the money.

At $400 a month, put $100 a week in that same box. You'll not only pay your payments, but you'll have $400 lift over at the end of the year to pay property taxes or to spend on Christmas.

If you have a car payment that should be operating for another four or five years, try this. Create a car payment to yourself by putting $100 a week into a savings account. When you have enough, go pay cash for the car. You'll save $4600 in interest on a $20,000 car. You say you can't save that much. Well, you can't afford a new car. Simple, huh?

Be realistic, and do your homework. A new car at $400 a month will cost you an additional $75 a month for taxes and insurance. Now your daily car payment is $15.62. That's 40% of your take-home pay if you make $400 a week. At earnings of $400 a week, a $270 monthly payment (1/4 of your take-home pay) is all you can afford. That means Kia, not a Honda.

Here's a formula for calculating how much your monthly payments amount to on a daily basis. For each monthly payment, multiply it times .032875. This tells you how much you owe each day, seven days a week for that payment.

Now, add up your daily totals. For weekly bills, use .142857 for the factor. For bills due once a year, use .002740. For bills due once per six months, use. .005480. I know you don't like that much math. I'm just trying to impress on you that if your daily bills add up to more than your weekly take-home pay divided by 7, you're in over your head.

If you keep a pad with you, record daily your expenses. Some days, it's terrifying to see what you owe. You don't live a day that you don't owe money. Even if you sit at home in the dark, your daily bills still add up.

So, think of paying those bills on a daily basis or weekly basis. You'll get a better insight of your financial status, and it'll teach you that bills are due at a specific time, but they're owed daily.

ADD IT UP FOR THREE MONTHS.

A very close friend called me one night asking for some financial advice. His money problems had plagued him for a long time. He couldn't figure out why they couldn't pay bills on time when he and she worked, and she received child support.

They rented a small mobile home, had no car payment, but still couldn't make ends meet. It seemed that bills were still unpaid when the money ran out. Both were paid on a weekly basis, and the child support was received weekly.

I asked him if he would do a little experiment to see where his money was being spent. He agreed. I told him to get a pad and list everything they spent money on for three months. This meant big bills, little bills, small purchases, everything. He decided to try it since nothing else seemed to work.

After three months, he brought his list to me, and we sat and discussed it in depth. After a few minutes, I noticed that some expenses we all incur were not on the list. I asked him about the trips to the store at night for milk, bread, etc. I also asked about hair cuts and beauty shop trips. He explained that these weren't weekly or monthly bills, that they happened only occasionally. Several other "occasional" things were not on the list, either.

When we estimated the "occasional" things left off the list, we saw a pattern of excessive, compulsory spending on things not needed and not necessary since they kept him from paying bills owed. The net difference in your incoming and outgoing income is your balance. If your balance is a negative and not a positive, you must change your spending habits to correct the situation. There are two ways to come out ahead. The first is to bring home more money than you owe or spend. The second is to owe less than you bring home. They're the same, right? Not quite. You can control what you spend a lot more than how much you bring home.

The spending part is the one you must control to come out ahead. Then, you must allow some of the money left for expenses that will come later, things like tires for the car, unexpected doctor visits, etc.

When we marked out things keeping him from at least breaking even, they would have money left, even without the child support, and without the overtime he was working. He was amazed. Now came the dedication on his part to let the spouse know of the new plan to put them on the positive side of the ledger. He and she must say "no" to those things that would hinder their normal bills from being paid.

They realized they had cable television and did not need to rent $20 worth of videos a week, order delivered pizza twice a week, smoke quite so much, make unnecessary trips to the store at night and other things that ate into their income and kept them unhappy. Taking lunch instead of eating from vending machines also helped.

I explained that bills came first. The plan worked for a while. They're now back in the same old rut, fussing at each other about money instead of sitting down for a family discussion to fix the problem.

Money causes more divorces than that cute little thing next door. When married, both must work together to formulate a spending plan and stick to it. Try this for three months. Only spend money on bills you owe. Don't buy anything you don't need. You'll be amazed at the difference in your cash flow.

LIFE WITHOUT AN SUV

Look into any garage or parking lot and calculate the number of suv's parked there. Some look like glorified pickup trucks, some like streamlined vans, small buses, or like big hotel rooms. The United States has come to an era of "we must have an suv". If you have one, don't feel offended by my writing. I just want to get you to think of why you bought it, how you can pay for it, and what life would be like without it.

They're called sport utility vehicles. Let's examine this for a minute. You need a vehicle. That is a known. Are you into sports? If so, does it call for a sport vehicle? How about the utility part? Utility means out of the normal use of a vehicle. Does utility mean to buy groceries, pick up the kids from school or carry the dog to the vet?

You see some suv's that must weigh 6,000 pounds. Imagine getting hit with that head-on. Some require athletic skills just to reach the driver's seat. I saw a young lady trying to get into one at the bank. She was about five feet tall. I had the fortunate opportunity not to see her try to get back to the ground. Some are so large you can't see around or over them when driving behind them.

AT my bank, the parking lot looks like a car lot of suv's. Everybody has to have one. The cost associated with these big gas-guzzling monsters must be astounding. Add your cost up sometime. Maybe you're perfectly happy with yours, but I prefer not to spend $850 a month for payments, tax, insurance and fuel. You could drive a Lexus for that amount of money.

If everyone had one, the parking stripes would have to be widened, roads made wider and even cdl licenses issued to drivers. One of the plus things about owning an suv is that unless it turns over, you're safer in them. They'd plow right over most cars and small trucks. But, two suv's hitting head-on at sixty miles per hour

21

would have the force of two normal cars hitting at one hundred miles per hour. Imagine that.

I know, I know. We're in America. We can drive anything we want. But at least give a little thought to hybrid cars or maybe a nice Chevy Impala like mine, or even a 4-door pickup truck. You could still carry groceries, take kids to school, go on a vacation and other things we Americans have come to believe are just normal activities.

Go ahead. Go out and buy one of those oversized individual buses with tv's, vcr's, etc. Keep those kids of yours entertained until you get home and let them get to their tv's, vcr's, etc. again. It's just my humble opinion that the cost of buying and keeping an suv is taking money from your retirement fund. You surely won't want one of those things when you retire. You'll need a good neighbor to help you into it, an American Express card to pay for gas and better vision than you'll have then to find your way around town or down the road.

A BUDGET? WHAT'S THAT?

Some say a budget is a way to go broke methodically. Ask someone if they have a budget, and watch them look at you funny. They'll say no 90% of the time. Ask if they go by a budget all the time. Almost none have or uses a budget.

If you take a vacation, you calculate each expense you think you'll have so you'll know how much money to take. Then, you find you didn't guess correctly, that you spent money on things you had not counted on. This is an example of budgeting.

You budget for a vacation, a trip to see a professional sporting event, etc. So, why not budget for your everyday expenses the same way? For some, a budget wouldn't make any difference in their spending habits at all. To others, it would reveal expenses they wouldn't want to admit they have.

If you can budget for one day, you can budget for a week, a month, a year or longer. If you don't anticipate your expenses, you can't know what your over-spending on. If you have a computer, go to Excel and type in months across the top, expenses down the left column. Show everything, even miscellaneous expenses that happen at unanticipated times. Eventually, you're going to incur those expenses, and you have to accumulate money before that time to be ready to pay when the time comes. If you don't have a computer, a tablet will do.

Do you have any idea how much you spend each day? It's true that some days you spend a lot more than others. But you must look at the total amount spent in a week, a month or year to realize that somewhere and sometime you spent a lot more than you thought or can remember.

Let's look at the math. If you spend $1 a day on soda drinks from the vending machine and you work 250 days a year, you spend $250 a year on this item. If you

23

buy a 12-pack on sale for $3, you'll save $125 a year, enough to pay your water bills all year. Of course, some of you will say that means you can drink twice as much now for the same money since they're cheaper. You're back where you started, the reason you can't get ahead.

The prior example is only one of the dozens of things you can save money on. Pool all of these savings, and you've got more in the bank instead of helping build other's accounts.

At work, a friend and I take turns cooking weekly. We have an electric skillet and the necessary supplies. It takes only minutes to cook for the two of us. We save a lot of money and eat well, too.

Years ago, I bought a small compact refrigerator (sits on my file cabinet in my office). Just the savings on soft drinks paid for it in eight months. Now, others are keeping their drinks there, too.

Going out for lunch can cost up to $1500 a year for fast food alone. Cooking lunch or taking a lunch could save $750 a year, enough to pay for that vacation you probably can't afford.

Do a budget. Plan smartly. Look at the numbers. They read like a book and dictate your trip to the "poorhouse" or your smart spending that you can pass on to the kids and theirs.

SPEND PAPER MONEY ONLY.

Try to guess how much change you have in your pocket or purse right now. More than $1 is too much. At times, my wife dumps her purse and finds several dollars in change.

Try this for a month. No matter what you pay for, pay with paper money, no coins. Every night, put all your coins into jars. At the end of the month, count all your change. Roll it and put it away until you have enough to make a bank deposit or buy something you need. You'll be amazed at the amount of change you can save. You could do this for a year and pay for most of your Christmas gifts.

Even better, if you can afford it, save the pocket change and $1 bills each night. The amount is unbelievable. Most would save $750 to $1000 a year. Not a bad way to pay those property taxes or homeowner's insurance premiums.

If someone gave you a choice of taking $1 million or take one penny the first day, then doubling it each day for the next 50 days, which would you choose? Look at the table below that doubles a penny for 50 days. It's hard to believe, right? Now, your coins in a jar aren't going to do this, but they will add up much quicker than you would have ever believed possible.

After looking at the chart, think of how many days you could double a penny each day.

1	$.01
2	$.02
3	$.04
4	$.08
5	$.16
6	$.32

7	$.64
8	$1.28
9	$2.56
10	$5.12
11	$10.24
12	$20.48
13	$40.96
14	$81.92
15	$163.84
16	$327.68
17	$655.36
18	$1,310.72
19	$2,621.44
20	$5,242.88
21	$10,485.76
22	$20,971.52
23	$41,943.04
24	$83,886.08
25	$167,772.16
26	$335,544.32
27	$671,088.64
28	$1,342,177.28
29	$2,684,354.56
30	$5,368,709.12
31	$10,737,418.24
32	$21,474,836.48
33	$42,949,672.96
34	$85,899,345.92
35	$171,798,691.84
36	$343,597,383.68
37	$687,194,767.36
38	$1,374,389,534.72
39	$2,748,779,069.44
40	$5,497,558,138.88
41	$10,995,116,277.76
42	$21,990,232,555.52
43	$43,980,465,111.04
44	$87,960,930,222.08
45	$175,921,860,444.16
46	$351,843,720,888.32
47	$703,687,441,776.64

48	$1,407,374,883,553.28
49	$2,814,749,767,106.56
50	$5,629,499,534,213.12

WHERE DID IT GO?

We've all done it. You look in your wallet or purse to see how much money you have and are amazed to see that some has disappeared, vanished, completely left the Earth. The first thing you do is ask where it went. You know you had more than that in there when you last looked.

Some even blame spouses or other family members with taking their money. Every-body's to blame but you, the caretaker of the smallest bank vault around, your wallet or purse. Your wallet or purse is your own personal, full time bank vault. You simply open it, remove a quantity of your wealth and hand it over to an eager sales-person willing to exchange something you may or may not need at all for it.

The problem with your vault is that it doesn't have a timer on it like the vault at the bank. It's not impossible to open until the designated time the next morning. You can open it at any time and any place and take a withdrawal from it.

After removing the money from your vault, you go to another location and do the same thing, over and over until your vault is either empty or in a seriously depleted state. You go home with all the stuff you've traded your money for. Later, you open your vault and discover a lot of money is missing, more than you can account for.

After interrogating your wife, kids and invisible people within your house, you sit and think of where you were and how much you spent. If you can't remember what you spent all the money on, you didn't need that stuff. It doesn't fit into your survival needs.

I just mentioned the word need. Almost always, needs are less than wants. Wants usually result in opening your vault too many times to buy things you don't need. A good salesperson is one who can sell you something you don't need at a price you can't afford.

So, the next time you look into your vault and ask where it went, trace your path to the places where you spent money to buy things you didn't need. If all else fails, simply write down on a pad each expense and save the ranting and raving sessions that keep the entire family upset for weeks.

Maybe you should put an invisible lock on your wallet or purse and pretend it won't open until you really need to spend money from it. Discipline never hurt anyone.

I DON'T HAVE TIME TO THINK ABOUT THE FUTURE.

Webster says the word "future" means: time that is to come, what is going to happen, an expectation of advancement or progressive development. He also says "futureless" means: having no prospect of the future success. He also says "future perfect" means: completion of an action by a specific time that is yet to come.

So, what' in your future? Do you think about the time still to come when you're closer to your retirement? Do you ever wonder what is going to happen? Have you accepted the fact that you will be futureless? Do you have a prospect of future success? Do you have future perfect plans to be at another financial level by a specific time?

We plan to go on vacations, go on a hunting trip, or maybe a weekend in the mount-aims. Do we plan to have enough money to enable us to do these things? Sure we do. But, do you ever wonder how you'll afford a home, send a child to college; those future things a little further away?

We must set goals for financial success as surely as we set goals to do other things. What is financial success to you? Is it just getting by, having the car payment at month end or paying the mortgage off early? Or does it mean setting a long- range plan to be where you want to be at a time that is specific?

Unless you win the lottery, saving is a long, slow process that requires patience, determination and perseverance. It requires learning how to do it, why to do it and the results at that projected time in the future.

What does success mean to you? I've known many successful people who never made a lot of money in their lives. I know people who have made a lot of money in their lives, but they never had a plan to improve their future, and end up totally broke.

When you go to the register to pay and get the urge to buy 5, 10, or 20 lottery tickets, go home and put the amount you didn't spend in a safe place. After a few months, you'll feel as if you had won the lottery. You'll be amazed at the amount and how fast it adds up.

Another way to save is to create another bill in your mind. Think as if you now owe $100 a month for it. Save $25 a week, and put it into a savings account. Every five months, convert it to a CD, and don't touch it. Make the bill one that never gets paid off. You'll be putting $1300 a year into CD's. Or put the money in an IRA each year. You'll earn some interest on it, and you get a tax deduction on the amount you invested, up to a certain amount limited by the IRS.

Unless you did, the future is yet to come. Penny-wise means: wise or prudent only in small matters. John Wayne said, "Life is tough. Life is tougher if you're stupid."

BUT I DON'T KNOW HOW TO ARBITRATE FOR A NEW CAR.

Are you one of those people who tremble at the thought of facing a car salesperson to purchase that American dream called an automobile? You're not alone. People view this process as if it were a primitive form of war. In reality, that's not too far fetched.

The salesperson has been thoroughly trained in intimidation, arbitration, math tricks and other things to take you to the cleaners. To the salesperson, it is a test of his man-hood or her womanhood. He's betting he can get inside your head, make you fall in love with the car, and then get you to sign a contract while he swells inside with the feeling he has won again. You're just out to buy a car, and you need to get battle-ready to prepare yourself for the big event.

If you're not computer literate, get help from someone who is. There are web-sites that show you the car you want, equipped the way you want it, the msrp (manufacturer's suggested retail price), the dealer invoice amount and other things. With this knowledge, you're ready to meet the other warrior, the salesperson.

When he tells you your numbers are way off base, ignore him. Only ask about dealer incentives, factory rebates and holding fees. Do the math with him. Don't trust him. You can add and subtract, but take a small calculator with you. Know before you meet him what the payments will be for a certain amount financed. If you know things like payment dollars per one thousand dollars financed, you can quickly calculate the full payment.

Remember, the salesperson must get approval from the sales manager, the other person sitting back there in a little room waiting for the salesperson to bring him an offer he'll likely refuse two or three times. The sales manager has risen through the ranks of salesperson to the position of being the final authority for the purchase price. Hold firm to your best offer no matter how defensive the salesperson gets. They'll try to make you think they're losing money. Believe me, they're not. The guy selling you the car will probably get a free vacation out of the deal.

The salesperson's job is to milk you for all he can, sell you an extended warranty, undercoating and other stuff that will increase your payments. Your job is to get the best deal you can live with. Over half of those who purchase new cars walk out of the dealer-ship with higher payments than they said they could afford. All those little extras add up.

You can arbitrate for that new vehicle. You just have to level the playing field, taking away the advantage from the salesperson and sales manager. Remember, you can always just turn and walk away and not lose anything but time. Then you can go to another dealer and start the process again. With practice, you can get better at this game.

A factory rebate is not a dealer discount. It is taken after your best deal. And, if you get a good deal, arbitrate for a good interest rate. After all, the average finance charge on a new vehicle is about $5000 during a 60-month loan, about $83 monthly in interest.

You should always hire somebody like me to research your car, make the deal for you and make the deal for you for a percent of the difference between the msrp and your price paid for the car.

So, get out there and show them you mean business. You'll be proud of yourself and even show your kids how it's done. They're going to need all the help they can get.

SHOULD MY WIFE WORK?

Years ago, I calculated the net take-home pay for my wife if she chose to work outside the home. The answer amazed me.

Believe me or not, there is a "cost" associated to working. Where do you think all those ladies at the bank get all those pretty dresses and that SUV parked out back? Those go-out-to-lunch costs add up, too.

For her to have a job would require another car, more clothing, higher eating costs, and the associated costs of the second vehicle. Another automobile would cost at least $18,000, along with it a monthly payment of $318. The tag and tax on the car would be about$8 a month. The insurance alone would be about $40 a month. Add $70 for lunch out, $90 a month for gas. Clothing expense would be about $40 a month, considerable more for those ladies who just can't be seen twice a month in the same dress. The cost of working is now up to $600 a month. Add another $128 monthly for putting us into another tax bracket. We now determine that the cost of working is about $725 a month.

With an hourly rate of $10, $1730 monthly, she'd take home about $1170, less the $728 cost of working, for a net of $442 a month, or $2.55 an hour. This is about 1/3 of minimum pay.

I'm not advocating that all women should or can stay at home instead of holding a job. There are exceptions. Those with two or three kids say they have to. They should add up the cost of working, though. When the above expenses are added to the cost of child-care, they may then decide that it's easier to stay at home and maybe pick up a few dollars with a craft hobby or even keeping another couple of kids.

If working wives could ride-share, carry a bag lunch, stay out of the clothing stores; it may prove beneficial to work at a job. It's not the business of anyone if you wear the same dress twice a week. After all, you paid for them.

I know what you're thinking. I can't leave my wife home without a car. If you'll plan grocery buying and other trips, you can do them when you're not working. Maybe she can drop you off at work at times to use the car.

Making a living financially doesn't depend only on the amount of money you earn. I recently heard a news report that said that 60% of people live paycheck-to-paycheck, and 50% of them earn from $50,000 to $100,000 yearly. This is absurd. Getting set up to live within your means takes a lot of courage, dedication and the mind-set most people don't have. As long as the "make money, spend money" attitude persists, you'll never get ahead financially.

TRUE OR FALSE TEST

Mark a t or f beside the following and then decide why you did it and what you'll do about it.

$10 a week is $520 a year.
5% of my paycheck=a week's pay every 4.6 months.
$5 in a jar is better than $5 in lottery tickets.
I can save 5% of my take home pay.
(2) $.50 drinks a day=$365 a year.
I know how much money I have in my pocket right now.
I pay too much by buying name brand products
I know how much I make before deductions.
I put all I can afford into my retirement plan at work.
I stock up on bargain sales.
I could live on 80% of my pay if I had to.
I have prescriptions filled December 31 to avoid deductibles.
If I was out of work for one month, I could pay my bills.
I pay only the minimum payment on my credit card balances.
I use a credit card because I don't have money to buy things.
My car payment is more than my house payment.
I buy name brands 100% of the time.
My $2000 car is fully insured with comprehensive insurance.
I buy high priced watches instead of cheaper ones.
I buy cheap shoes to save money.
My hot water heater is set at more than 115 degrees.
In summer, my thermostat is set at lower than 75 degrees.
In winter, my thermostat is set at higher than 68 degrees.
I get a soft drink from a vending machine after grocery shopping.
I carry snacks and cold drinks while on a trip.
My mortgage rate is more than 2% higher than the current rate offered.

I buy 93-octane gas, but my owner's manual says 87-octane will work in my car.

I have a big screen television in a living room of less than 120 square feet.

I smoke, but I can't afford groceries.

I don't service my car. I just wait for it to break down and fix it.

My truck's stereo and wheels are worth more than the truck.

I turn off lights when leaving a room for a while.

I don't service my lawn mower. I just fix it when it needs repair.

I play golf, but I can't afford gas to get to work.

I get a big tax refund, loaning the government money interest free for the year.

I don't make plans for trips to town. I just go when I need things.

I don't save change, wrap and deposit it.

I don't invest in a retirement plan at work.

I carry a lot of money with me all the time.

I buy Christmas gifts with a credit card, then pay minimum payments monthly.

MOM, I'VE GOT TO HAVE THAT.

You and I know that our wants far exceed our needs. No, I don't mean we should do without everything. I'm talking about things you want on the spur of the minute that won't appeal to you at all 24 hours later.

Kids are the most obvious ones to say, "I've got to have that". Then there are the big kids, those grown people who think the moment at hand is all that counts, and that the future will take care of itself.

My advice is that when you see a car, a house, a gun, clothing, etc., you just have to have, just simply turn and walk away. Ask yourself if it really means that much to you. Ask if the cost of it will deprive you of your next meal or tank of gas. Whatever it cost, if a small item or large, go home and put one-half of the cost of it into a jar. You'll save some money and still have some left for the next "I'll die if I don't get that".

I know a family who has a mobile home because they can't afford a down payment for a conventional home. I'm not knocking mobile homes. I've owned two of them myself. I'm simply making the point that if they didn't have two vehicles, two four-wheelers, all the deer hunting equipment known to man, a big dog that eats more than a human, a boat and other self-declared necessities, maybe they could have afforded the down payment on a conventional home. They made choices that will affect them for the next thirty years, then the rest of their lives.

I was in a large toy store, a big chain store. A young woman with a four-year old son in a buggy in front of me created quite a stir. The kid was knocking things off every row of toys. He was yelling, "I want it". Instead of giving him a lesson I learned when I was taken outside of the church, she just smiled and picked up the items from the floor. The child learned only that eventually his mom would buy him whatever he wanted. The mom didn't know what to do or she wouldn't have taken him in there in the first place.

I saw a car on a lot once that literally turned me into a child wanting that red sucker in the jar. I had to have that car. I went home and asked myself a lot of questions. Do I need to trade cars? Can I afford this car? Will insurance and taxes be more? Will I get enough trade from my old car? Can I afford to pay big payments for sixty months? Reality set in. The want was still there, but it wasn't pulling at me as before.

I got a pad, pen and calculator and did a budget for the next year, month by month. I still owed a balance on my home. I calculated that if I could afford the car, I'd simply pay extra on the house payment until it was paid for.

After fifteen months, I paid off the house mortgage, sold instead of trading my car, put the money from my car and then some toward the purchase of the new car I just had to have. The car payment was less than the house payment had been. I was spend zero on car maintenance, got better gas mileage, had my home paid for, and saved money.

Think it out. Plan, wait, calculate and set a plan to accomplish your goal. Don't get nervous every time you see something you can't live without. It would cost you dearly and prevent you from progressing toward your financial goals, retirement, etc.

DOES A DOLLAR GO AS FAR AS IT DID?

Why does a dollar seem not to go as far as it did years ago? Is it that everything costs more now? Is it a result of impulse buying? Let's look into this problem.

The average cost of gasoline is around $1.30 per gallon. In 1959, it cost $.27 a gallon. That's 4.8 times more today than in 1959. Compare the amount of money you earn today with earnings in 1959. Today, the average earnings may be $30,000 per household. In 1959 it may have been about $2800. That means you earn 10.7 times more today than a person would earn in 1959. Do the math. Gasoline at $1.30 per gallon is 2.2 times less today than in 1959 compared to earnings. We seem to drive more and longer, too.

Think about the cost of bread, milk, sugar, eggs, flour, mayonnaise, jelly, chicken, etc. Some of these items cost less than three times what they cost in 1959. And most people continue to think the cost of things take a bigger % of their paychecks. It's not true.

So, ask yourself, "Why can't I buy as much for a dollar now"? The answer is that you can and do buy more of a specific item for a dollar now. So, let's get to the real problem that plagues most people today.

Think of what kind of things you purchased or spent money on years ago. You buy or spend today based on your inability to say "No". You impulse buy all kinds of things at those "last chance" counters before exiting the stores. You think you just have to have things that others have or that you're bombarded with on television, newspapers and radio.

If you'd simply go for one month without buying those things you don't need or have to have, it would amaze you how much more money you would have left.

Another test would be to carry a small pad and pen with you for a month. Record every penny you spend, no matter if it's a penny or ten dollars. After a month, add it up. Look at what took your money. Now, sell all that junk you didn't need at a flea market, and get part of your money back.

I see people driving up to the front of a grocery store, get out and pay $.75-$1.00 for a soft drink from a vending machine. At times, the same store sells such drinks for as little as $.17 each. You say, "But I wanted a cold drink". So, carry a small six pack cooler with you with two of those gel freeze packs from your freezer.

I see people at work spend $2-$3 a day in vending machines. Years ago, I bought a small refrigerator for my office. I store drinks, food for lunch, etc., and paid for it quickly with the savings.

I have an electric skillet in my office. My friend, Rick, and I take turns weekly bringing food and cooking lunch. The next office has a toaster and a microwave oven. Laura is nice enough to let us use it. We eat well and cheaper and don't lose hours away from work, not to speak of gas to go out.

BUT I'VE GOT A SAVINGS ACCOUNT.

About 40 years ago, banks charged 8% interest on loans and gave 5% interest on savings accounts. Today, you'll get charged about 12% interest on a loan, but you'll only get about 0.7% interest on your savings account. All those "free" banking fringes aren't exactly free, are they?

Many people have savings accounts. There may be a dozen different types of accounts out there. A regular passbook savings account may pay 1% interest. If you put $200 into such an account and leave it for 20 years, it will yield $86.68 in interest, and your account total will be at a total of $286.68. If you put that same $200 in a money market account at an annual gain of 10% for 20 years, you'll gain $1267.72 and see a total of $1467.72.

If you used that same $200 to make craft projects and sell them for $500 in one month, you gain four times more than if you had invested it for 20 years in money markets.

If banks can give you 0.8% interest on your savings account and charge you 12% on loans, who is making all the money? Add the fact that you pay income tax on your savings account interest, and you'll net about 0.6%.

Don't get me wrong. Saving money if good. If you don't trust stocks, money markets, etc., use a CD (certificate of deposit). You can get them for 5 years, 3 years, 1 year, 10 months, or less. If you don't want your money were you can't get to it quickly, don't worry. You only lose the interest on the month in which you withdraw it.

Ask yourself why you want to save money. How much will you save? For what length of time will you save it?

I had a friend who got so upset about paying 15% federal tax on interest from his savings he withdrew half of the money and kept it at home. Think for a moment about what he did. For $100 in the account, he received $3 interest. His tax on the interest was $.45. He realized a $2.55 gain after taxes. By keeping it hidden at home, he gained nothing. He also took the risk of fire destroying it. Uncle Sam lost, and he lost. When money stops circulating, everybody loses.

The definition of save is: to keep from being spend or lost; to secure from waste or expenditure: to lay up: to reserve.

I like the "to secure from waste" part. Why? That's what keeps most people from saving money. The "to keep from being spent" part doesn't sound right since saving it to spend later may be your mission. If your savings account is in the bank, a piggy bank, a drawer, etc., good for you. Something is always better than nothing.

When my 8-year old grandson wanted to go to Walmart, he would get me to pay for his toys. When I asked why he didn't spend his allowance money, he said, "That's my money". It took me a while to see he was already practicing good money habits at such an early age.

When you spend, ask yourself if it makes sense. You may talk yourself out of it more times than you'd like to think.

JUST WHERE IS THE POORHOUSE?

Your vision of a poorhouse may be a large white house sitting on a hill in the country, with a white picket fence and a porch full of rocking chairs all around it.

Actually, the poorhouse could be the house you retire in and have paid on for 30 years. If you don't handle your money correctly, your house becomes a "poorhouse" by the time you retire. Some don't have to wait until retirement. They may be middle age or even younger. They are up to their eyeballs in debt and can't see any way out.

Or it could be a large cardboard box or a back alley in a large city. People in this situation aren't only down on their luck. They may include those who failed to plan during their working years and simply ran out of time. You see, if you simply add up all the non-essential things you spend money on along the way, you'd be amazed at how much money it adds up to.

If you work 45 years and spend $20 a week on such things, you've spent $41,600. If you had put this into CD's at 4.5%, you'd have $152,000 after 45 years. You could then withdraw $700-$800 each month for life to help with expenses. Start at age 20 to put $100 monthly into a retirement plan, and you'd probably have about $215,000 at age 65. It adds up, huh?

BUT, IT'S FREE.

We've all received those "free" offers in the mail. Remember, nothing is free. It costs something to make that "whatever it is".

I recently received a mailing to get a "free" monthly planner and daily records book. The planner was valued at over $23. The records book was worth $12. All I had to do was send $6 for postage and handling. Both items looked nice. For a moment, I was tempted. I thought I didn't need them, but that they were a bargain. Then, I thought, "If it was two mailboxes for the price of one, would I need the extra one"?

My brain finally caught up with my mind, and I decided that I didn't want to decrease my bank account by $6 for something I can easily do without. I could buy four gallons of gas. Then I could drive 100 miles "free". There I go again. Nothing's free. I read a sign that said, "Buy the first item at double the regular price, and get the second item of the same or less cost absolutely "free". I'm sure some people fell for this one.

As a young boy, I was in a grocery store with my mother. I was looking at the big red apples in the bin. A store employee said, "They're $.10 each or two for $.25". A guy behind me said, "I'll take two". I was amazed that the guy didn't figure this out. What a rip-off.

When someone in the business of selling tells you "This is free", put one hand over your wallet and the other on your car keys. Then get out of there. If this person is making money by giving stuff away, let me know how he does it. Some of you will say, "It's on volume".

Free shipping can also be a rip-off. When you see that claim, you can bet your bass boat the price has been jacked up, possibly more than you'd normally pay.

Free-shipped items may show a regular shipping fee of $6.95, even though it actually costs about $1.00 to ship it. Watch out for the shipping and handling. Shipping may be reasonable, but handling charges can be what it cost Joey to pick it up from inventory, Suzy to do the paper-work and Bob to count the money he'll make by selling you a bargain. The handling cost more than pays for the labor cost to the company.

We all get mail saying, "Free, free, free". When you get such mail, roll it up into a ball. Take a "free" shot into the trash container. Your wife will be proud of you, and the practice won't hurt.

If you feel all those "free" things are really "free", go ahead and accept them. Then, take them to a flea market and sell them. The proceeds will pay 60% of your cost, and your credit card balance grows 40% plus finance charges.

When I was twenty, an encyclopedia salesman "gave" me a set of books because my neighbors chose me to get the "free" set. I paid about $325 for them and learned a life lesson.

A cosmetic salesman came to my door with a hand full of his products. I opened the door to hear him say, "These are free". I immediately took them, thanked him, and shut the door. That guy stood on my porch, looking at his empty hands, stared with a blank expression, then slowly walked to his car. I'm sure his speech was changed before the next sales pitch.

I remember a joke about a Teaberry Coffee salesman. He would arrive at a home and give his pitch as "Good afternoon madam. I represent the Teaberry Coffee Company. Today, and only today, the Teaberry Coffee Company is offering a free slop-jar (bed pan) for each pound of Teaberry coffee you buy". He walked for hours, knocked on thirty doors, and sold one pound of Teaberry coffee. He came upon a huge boarding house with 720 rooms and delivered his pitch to the landlord. The landlord said, "Wait a minute. If I buy 720 pounds of Teaberry coffee, the Teaberry Coffee Company will give me 720 brand new slop jars"? The salesman gulped and said, "Wait a minute, lady. That is an order. The Teaberry Coffee Company may just want to build you a big outhouse out back there".

ARE YOU A SPENDER OR A SAVER?

Are you saving for a rainy day, saving for that something special, or not saving at all? One person is a saver and another a spender, probably deeply rooted from their child-hood.

Give one child a dollar, and they'll spend it in thirty minutes. Give a dollar to another, and they'll put it in their secret hiding place, anxiously awaiting the next dollar to be placed with it.

When raising children, convince them of how many hours a month you must work to pay for that car they use for their pleasure times. Don't let them believe somehow that it came from the car fairy. Children need to learn early in life why we work, why we spend, why we save and then the consequences of each.

So, why does a spender spend? Emotions may play a bigger role than habit. Whether you're a saver or a spender has nothing to do with how much money you have. Wealthy people pinch the pennies, and rich people know how to spend wisely.

The fear of not having enough inspires one person to save and another to spend it foolishly, no matter how much money they have. Even rich people sometimes have to be taught to save.

Every time I say I'm going to win the sweepstakes, my wife says, " How much do you need"? Our culture wants us to believe we don't have enough. Unless you travel extensively or just want to accumulate land, houses, etc., how much does it take for you to feel secure?

Emotional needs aren't always our reasons for spending. It may just be a bad habit. If you grew up in a family that ate junk food and fast foods, you'd probably

47

do that too after you're grown.

How do you become a saver? Learning to save is that you want to save more than you want to spend. It's like the kid that saved gas money for years before he became sixteen because he wanted to drive a car so badly. If we want something more than other things, we'd start saving for it. So, it's not all discipline. It's that desire for something that forces us to save.

What are you saving for? Is it a car, a home, or new furniture? Is it for a three-day vacation? Is it for that $500 gun you must have? It doesn't matter as long as you save.

Saving is more fun than spending. You then feel in control of your money and your life. When you have thirty pounds of pennies, about $30, roll them and lug them to the bank and deposit them. Rolling dimes, nickels and quarters can me more exciting. Every day, empty all your change to different jars, and watch them grow.

You say you can't save money from your little paycheck. You've heard that, right? The amount you save has little to do with your income. It has to do with whether you truly want to save and if you're willing to adjust your lifestyle to do so. Some people who don't earn much money save more than those who earn a lot. Why? It's because they're not convinced they need three cars, a 3000 square foot home, a boat and motor, a jet ski or a $400 dog. Then, what is the key? The key is spending less than you earn. It's simple, right?

Earning money is a necessity if uncle Henry didn't leave you his fortune. Managing that money is quite different. People don't know enough about their own financial reality. They can't tell you how much they earn. They don't know what it takes to make a living. They don't know their discretionary income. You think I'm kidding? How much do you earn monthly within $50? That was hard, huh?

Educate yourself. Sit down and look at your bills and statements and calculate your income and outgo. Do you like what you see? If not, seek out a way to change it. You must either earn more money or spend less. Spending less is easier. Ask yourself how you want to use your money, how you want to live, and where you are financially. Managing money requires time. Set aside that time monthly. To stay on track, I some-times sit and calculate my income and bills for as far as four years ahead.

A credit card is not a borrowing tool. It's a cash management tool. If you want to borrow, use a bank at 8-10%, not on a credit card at 20%+. When you use a credit card, you're spending tomorrow's money, losing more and more financial control and freedom. The bottom line is to stop spending.

Saving money isn't just dropping it into a piggy bank on the shelf. You can save by carpooling or using public transportation when feasible. Gas, insurance, maintenance cost, etc. is reduced dramatically. And you won't have to trade cars every four or five years.

The U.S. Bureau of Labor Statistics shows we spend $1850 a year on clothing and the upkeep. Buy from such stores as Walmart or similar discount stores. Buy a "good" pair of shoes. They cost more, but they'll last many times longer than that pair of bargain basement ones you get for about $9.99.

Best of all, save to cut up your credit cards. You need an emergency fund to handle unexpected expenses. You then become your own lending agency at 0% interest. If you have a credit card balance of $8500, your interest alone at 14% would be over $1000 a year. Saving money for buying those same things will eliminate the interest entirely.

Save for the time your kids are 13-16 years old. That's when music lessons, instruments, sports equipment, etc. will take a sizeable chunk of cash.

So, become a saver. Sure you'll have to spend, too. But spend wisely, and give yourself an attitude adjustment to redirect your saving and spending habits.

I saw an old movie that showed a fictional scene. When people obtained a certain age, about 70, they went into a hug building on a hill. Here, they were directed to a room with a table in the center of it, with movie screens around the room. The person got to choose his/her favorite music and scenery. Music would play, and the screens would show animals and birds or trees that at that time were extinct. The person would be given an injection and put to death. Folks, it isn't his easy. You'll get older and face your own "poorhouse" if you don't plan not to go there.

I'M NOT A COMPULSIVE SHOPPER, AM I?

The definition of compulsive is: the state of being compelled, a force or agency that compels, an irresistible impulse to perform an irrational act. You did see that word "irrational", didn't you?

The compulsive shopper believes that shopping will make them feel better. It actually makes them feel worse. Such shopping can be a seasonal balm for depression, anxiety and loneliness, especially during the Christmas season. The increased financial debt a person has created makes them feel worse.

Do you shop for a "pick-me-up"? Do you buy things you don't need? Do you have racks of clothing with price tags still on them? Do you go into a mall with the intention of buying a couple of items and come home with a bag full? Do you have problems with remembering when and where you purchased a particular item? Are you in denial about the problem of compulsive shopping? Do you take extra jobs to pay your bills? If so, you are a compulsive shopper.

I was in a women's clothing store with my wife and noticed a lady at the counter with a large stack of clothes on the counter. The clerk repeatedly told her one credit card after another was full and couldn't be used. The lady said that was okay, that she didn't need the clothes anyway. She left the store, probably feeling more depressed than ever.

How can you cure this condition? Addictive behaviors tend to congregate. You're not alone. So, search out a group that meets about shopping addiction. Many towns and cities have credit counseling centers that may help with the problem.

How do you prevent shopping binges? You can pay for purchases by check or cash. Make a shopping list, and buy only what is on the list. Keep only one credit card for emergence use only. Do the "window shopping" thing after stores close. Avoid phoning in a catalog order, and don't watch the home shopping channels. Take a walk or exercise when the urge to shop hits you. If you're out of control, seek counseling or find a support group.

Do you buy things on credit that you wouldn't pay cash for? Does spending money cause anxiety? Do you lie to others about what you buy or how much you spend? Do you spend time juggling accounts and bills to allow you to spend even more? The thrill of spending is short-lived. You feel worse within hours or even minutes.

Have you ever gone into a restaurant planning to get a cheap lunch or dinner and order the $10.95 special? We've all done it. Within minutes after eating, guilt sets in. You wished you had not ordered that expensive food, even though it tasted good at the time.

If you can't control your sudden urges to spend, go to one of those "everything's a dollar" stores. Look around for an hour and buy $5 worth. That's your limit. And there's a chance you found something you really needed and have been looking for.

BUT THERE ARE MORE PLACES TO SPEND MONEY NOW.

As a teenager in the fabulous 50's, I remember my small town having three gas stations. They all closed at about six pm. If you planned an out-of-town trip at night, you had to fill up before six pm.

Of course, there was no need for using a lot of gas because there were not a lot of places to go that would be open at night. That meant you didn't spend a lot of money. We couldn't go to the local convenience store at 9:30 for milk, snacks or gas.

At that time, we had only two restaurants, no fast food ones. And they closed about 8 pm. Of course, hamburgers and fries were cooked on the stove at home, not at the restaurant at four times the price.

Yeah, we hung out at these restaurants to talk and listen to the music. A shake would cost about $.25 and would last an hour or so.

Our local Walmart store is open 24/7. I can say that if anybody has the urge to go there at 3:10 am for any reason is out of touch with his senses. A little planning, like shopping at lunch or on the way home from work should avoid this type of childish behavior. Or even better, eat a good lunch on the money you would probably have wasted by shopping.

I can see the hands on the merchants with out-stretched fingers, begging us to patronize them. One local restaurant is surely luring us in by blowing the smell from the kitchen to the outside by means of some type of fan. When you ride by, the smell is so incredible you rarely can drive past it.

We've all seen the explosion of fast food places on the outskirts of small towns. As you ride by, there seems to be more than ever before, with bright lights and all types of signs to get us to stop. And when you do go inside, you'll pay more for a chicken sand-wich than for a whole chicken. A burger costs more than six of them off the backyard grill.

When I was a child, and I'd yell out "I'm hungry", my mother would either give me a piece of cake she had made from scratch or a peanut butter sandwich to quench the hunger pains. And if you were extremely hungry, a sliced banana on the peanut butter sandwich would do the trick. Of course, back then smooth peanut butter was our only choice.

As a teenager, a night out was rare unless you were dating. If lucky enough to have a date and borrow dad's car (teens didn't have their own cars), it meant a trip to the movies or to one of the two restaurants in town. If going out of town, you had to gas up the car early and not even count on going too far. Dad would check the mileage and calculate the cost of gas.

When I shop, I know exactly what I'm going to buy before I get to the store. I go in, walk to my item(s), pay for them and leave. When you get to the checkout, don't even give a glance at all the "you need this stuff" in shelves at the register. Just concentrate on how much you've already spent.

So, you now see that all you have to do to spend more money after dark is to get into your car and go to town. I just told you how to avoid spending more. Stay home. Don't go to town. No, you won't get $200 for going past "go". But, you'll save a few bucks and spend time with the family.

GRADUATING, BUT NOT READY?

I graduated from Trion, Georgia high school in 1961, a long time ago. Things are a lot more complicated now, but simple math is the same as it was then. Along the way, I learned hard lessons regarding money and making a living.

Many young people today graduate and can't use or don't use enough math skills to enable them to get through the daily use of money transactions. High school graduates know little or nothing about balancing a checkbook or how to set up a bank account.

Even colleges seem to teach world religions, world affairs, culture diversity and other things that won't teach you the complicated world of finances. Sure they teach math classes, but if the student learned all kinds of math, but not how to run his/her financial affairs; they're in trouble.

I remember when my son graduated from high school. He asked me to help him set up a bank checking account. I did, and he wrote seven checks the first day. Three of them were bad ones. I truly believe he thought he could write all the checks in any amount he wanted, and he'd be okay. I quickly baled him out and closed the account. He acted like he was dipping gold coins from a well. He's older now and is still learning lessons from his father.

If schools, especially colleges, can teach some of the stupid classes they teach, why not slip in a class on handling money, keeping a bank account or investing in the future.

Consider the math problem of "the missing dollar". Long ago, three brothers rented an apartment for a total of $30 a month. Each brother paid the landlord $10. The land-lord changed the rent to $25 monthly, giving $5 to their sister to be returned to the brothers. The sister didn't know how to divide $5 among three

54

brothers. She exchanged it for five $1 bills. She gave each brother $1 and she kept the last $2. At this point, each brother has paid $10 and gotten a refund of $1. This means the three brothers are out of pocket a total of $27, $9 each. The sister has the other $2. If $27 + $2 is $29, where is the missing dollar?

Most young people don't know the value of a dollar or how to make it last. It's your duty teach them. If you don't know yourself, learn; then teach the child. A college graduate has lived almost 30% of his life expectancy, has no work experience and no job when he/she graduates. Now, they're to hunt a job, make money, pay some debts and try to learn what school didn't teach them; how to manage their finances.

Managing money is a full time job. It doesn't take breaks. It doesn't go away. You must know how to do it and do it well to survive. Money can make you extremely happy or extremely miserable. Learn, unlearn and relearn until you get it right.

BUT I'VE JUST GOT TO TALK.

What the heck is this just-got-to-talk hysteria? It seems that over half of you are on one of those cute little cell phones, yapping your heads off about things you wouldn't necessarily talk about if you didn't have one of the things. About twenty percent of the cars on the road have someone inside on one of the things. They're acting like they can actually drive right and talk, too.

I was recently in a large home improvement store, about fourth in line to check out. The clerk was on her cell phone talking about refinancing her house. I patiently waited for about ten minutes before being checked out. I got home and called the store to talk to the manager. I told him of this stupid act by one of his clerks. He was outraged and hope-fully took care of it.

I see neighbors driving two blocks from their homes, and they're already on the cell phone. Make the call before you leave home or when you get home. These things aren't free, and the time used on them isn't either. One of my friends says his wife has one and actually uses up her 3600 minutes a month. That's 60 hours of talking and listening. That's 8% of your total time on this planet. What could she possibly talk about for that amount of time?

I work about thirteen miles from home. One evening on my way home, I was behind a good friend. He stopped at an intersection and sat and talked on his phone for two minutes. He never looked up or down the road. I blew my horn at him, and he proceeded into the highway. About half way home, I saw him run off the pavement twice, still on the phone. He still hadn't noticed who I was. When I allowed time for him to get home, I called him and told him if he couldn't talk and drive at the same time, he needed to not leave home or put the phone in the dash compartment. We're still friends.

I've been in meetings when cell phones would sound. This is a distraction for every-one. All the people in the meetings have office phones, e-mail and probably secretaries. If we're having that many emergencies, we're in trouble. If such people are that indispensable, their bosses are in trouble.

I played golf in a tournament once and was teamed with players I had never met. One young guy was on the cell phone at every tee box. He was calling his office to make sure everything was going well. This was absolutely unnecessary. If he didn't have someone at the office capable of filling in for him, he is a failure at delegating.

You've seen the television ads that tell you they'll give you phone service for $29.99 or as much as $44.95 if you've lost service due to not paying your bill on time. Are people really this messed up? It was all that talking that caused you the problem in the first place. You end up paying even more for these weird phone services than the one you couldn't afford. Cut down on the talking, and get your head back in order.

If you didn't have a cell phone to call home one hundred yards away to tell them you would be home in thirty seconds, would the call really be an emergency? If you need to call home to see what you need to pick up at the store, simply place a note in the car seat when you leave home. It's amazing what a little planning can do.

With some reported evidence that excessive cell phone usage could cause brain cancer, it appears we'll have only 5% of the population with enough sense to remember their way home.

If long distance calls are bulging your phone bill, make these calls at night or on the weekends when rates are lower. If you make a lot of such calls, consider getting an 800 service line. If you and your phone buddy have e-mail, try that.

If you stop thinking while talking, think that you learn more from listening than talking. If you just have to talk, do it without endangering our lives and ask yourself if all those calls are really necessary, or at least necessary at the time.

VISIT YOUR BANK FOR SOME GOOD ADVICE.

I've heard people say they have a checking account, a savings account and a Christmas club account at their bank. That's good, huh? Maybe it isn't.

If your bank takes fees from your checking account for not maintaining the minimum balance, for goodness sake, do whatever is necessary to get the balance above that amount. Banks pay interest on savings accounts or even on checking accounts, but the interest rate may be 0.5% or so. If your checking account fees are more than the interest you're getting on your savings account, transfer the latter to the former to avoid the fees. A Christmas club account pays almost no interest, but it's easy to have the money withdrawn from your paycheck, and it is nice to have a good check at Christmas to help with the expenses.

The other extreme would be to have thousands of dollars in the checking account paying 0.25% interest. Bank CD's have monthly, six month, ten month, one year or other terms of maturity. If you're building your checking account to several times your monthly expenses, transfer some to a CD account and earn many times the interest you would if left in the checking account. Of course, it takes patience and a willingness to leave the money there until it matures.

An IRA at your bank can save you substantial money. With the maximum deposit rates going up almost every year, and the fact that you don't pay tax at year-end on the money deposited, the tax savings and interest gains are sizeable. If a couple put $6000 into an IRA each year, and their tax bracket is in the 15% area, they could save $900 in federal taxes alone, probably about $300 in state taxes.

Don't strain your eyes for hours to read all that tiny print on the bank information material. Just go down to the bank and ask to talk to someone about your investments and how to make the most of them. There are people at all banks who can guide you and explain the process. Be sure to check out benefits for your age group. Special plans are available for seniors, too.

Of course, to do any of this, you first must make a dedicated effort to save some money in one or more plans. Use payroll deduction all possible. You don't miss the money and will adjust your living style in accordance, without touching your savings account.

Write all your questions on a piece of paper or on an index card. Sound like you know what you're talking about even if you don't. Set a date and time to go to the bank. Don't be ashamed or bashful. It's your money, and the bank will be happy to help you make it more so they can use it in their business. Get into the habit of saving in several ways. It's fun, too.

BUT SMALL CARS USE LESS GAS, DON'T THEY?

Years ago, when gasoline prices were raised to an all time high, some people actually went out and purchased small, high-mileage cars to offset the price of gas. Their state of mind was and still is questionable.

Let's do the math. If you drive 288 miles a week (15,000 a year), and your car's miles per gallon rating is 22; then you use 13 gallons of gas weekly. If the gas price increases from $1.15 to $1.50 a gallon, your increased gas cost would be $4.55 weekly, $19.72 monthly, and $232.60 a year. If you buy a small car at $17,000 and finance it, the payments would be about $375 a month. Financed at sixty months means you pay back $22,500 in five years. That would be an additional 15,000 gallons of gas. This means that five years of paying $.35 more a gallon would cost $1183, compared with $22,500 for that extra little car for five years. That's a no-brainer, right?

I was in Germany and drove on the super highway without speed limits. I was driving at about 95 miles per hour when ahead I saw a tiny car making its way off a ramp and onto the highway. It was one of those little East German cars, about the size of one I saw two clowns get out of at the circus.

I flew past that little puttering car and saw it shake and wobble. There appeared to be about four people in there. I can't imagine having a wreck in that little car. You'd be fused to it and probably buried with it.

When gasoline prices go up, think back. In 1959 when I got my first driving license, the cost was about $.25 a gallon. Today, it costs about $1.35, or 5.4 times more. Think of your hourly rate back in 1959 if you're old enough. If not, take my word for it that it was about $1.00 an hour. You probably earn 12-15 times that much now. So, gasoline prices, if following our earnings trend, would be about $3.38 a gallon now. Our problem is that even though gas is less than 50% of what it could be, we drive 3-4 times more now than then.

So, the next time you want to save money on gasoline, keep the old clunker and drive less by trip planning. Get gas either on your way to work or from work. Pick up other things you need then, too. Don't make an extra trip after you get home.

When the urge hits you to save money on your auto expense, go outside, wash your old car, grin and go back to your easy chair and remote.

KEEP IT, OR TRADE IT?

One of the strongest urges we experience next to bringing Cindy Crawford home for Christmas is to go downtown to trade for that hot, shiny new car.

The first thing you'll see is that finely tuned salesman walking toward you, grinning like the television evangelist asking for the largest gift you can possibly afford. His job is to tell you how great his new car is and how your run-down wreck may not get you back home.

Ask yourself why and how you got to this point. What made you decide to give up your daily companion for a fling with a beautiful, but untested new model? Is it because your older car doesn't love you anymore? No, it's probably because that shiny new car is drawing you into temptation.

If your reason for trading is that you are spending too much to keep your old car in running order, think again. If you've faithfully serviced that old car, you shouldn't have many problems with it.

If a transmission is needed at about $1500, this is equal to about 4 new car payments. Even if you replace a motor for about $2500, it is the same as about 6 new car payments. If you can't afford such repairs every six years, then you can't afford a new car payment. After all, that payment would cost the same as a new motor and transmission every nine months. That sounds strange, right? But, these are the facts.

If you have some patience before buying or trading for the new car, try these tricks. After you have had your car three years, pay $60 a month to yourself for a reserve for upcoming mechanical problems. It'll soften the blow when those times come. After your last payment is made, keep the old car, put $400 a month into a savings account. If you can't wait any longer than two years to get the new car, you've saved $9600 toward the down payment. Along with your trade, you've greatly reduced your next car payment. If you're very patient, you'll have enough to pay cash for the next car. But, if you can get 0% financing, put the money into CD's and make some interest on it.

If after four years with a car, you replace the cv boots, the cost would be about 1/3 the cost of joint repairs, oil changes, tire rotations and transmission work will also prevent large repair expenses later.

If you don't currently own a pickup trick, don't go out and buy one for the three trips a year to the home supplies store or to haul off brush from the lot twice a year. Renting a pickup makes more sense. You won't pay taxes, insurance or maintenance cost on it.

The same goes for buying a new car because your old one may not make it 1200 miles to grandma's house and back twice a year on that well-earned vacation. Rent a car or van, even an SUV. You get to drive a new vehicle and won't still owe for it later.

A good example of keeping it until it drops is the amazing number of old, very old pickup tricks on the road today. Some things never wear out on them, like headlights and blinkers. They're seldom used. An old truck without air conditioning or automatic transmission or all the other stuff should run for years and years if routing maintenance is performed.

When that new car urge grabs you, intimidates you, goes to bed with you, takes a shower with you or even when you're showing her how much you love her, simply sit down, grab the remote and watch a good western or auto repair show. The urge will go away or it will force you to town to meet the cheerful salesperson.

SAVING MONEY IN THE KITCHEN

You ask, "How can I save money in the kitchen"? Think about it. You have an oven, a refrigerator, a stove and maybe a microwave. If you don't own a microwave oven, get one now, preferably one with 1200 watts of power.

A microwave oven uses less power than a conventional oven, cooks many times faster and is said to cook food more uniformly and better than a conventional oven. You can keep the frozen dinners in your freezer and have a hot meal in minutes instead of using pots and pans, heating up the kitchen, pre-heating an oven and making a big mess on the top of the stove. Another plus for a microwave oven is that the more you have in your freezer, the easier it is to cool.

While a microwave oven is cooking your meal, typically in about five to eight minutes, you can do other chores without having to watch it cook on a stove or in a conventional oven. Then, you can actually eat out of the cooking container, saving on the amount of dishes you put into that dishwasher.

Unless you forget to punch holes in those potatoes, wieners, etc., you don't even have a mess to clean up. So, what have we learned about cooking with a microwave oven? We've saved time, money, power and hot water. That's not bad, huh?

If your stove's cooking eyes aren't the pulsing type, going on and off, you may want to invest in this type of stove.

If you have a can of biscuits and sausage links to cook, use the microwave oven to cook the sausage and a toaster oven to cook the biscuits. In ten minutes, you're sitting in your recliner, eating and watching Gunsmoke. This method of cooking saves using that big oven and stove. You've saved time and power again. Just a little planning of this type can add up to substantial money and time saved.

If you've got only a few dishes to wash, wash them in the sink. You save lots of water and power. A little work isn't bad for you, either. This choice may let those kids in the house know how it used to be done.

When purchasing new kitchen appliances, think about how you'll use them. If there's only one or two of you, you don't need a 29 cubic foot refrigerator-freezer as big as a car. Think about your eating habits, how much freezer space is needed and what you'll keep in it. You'll pay dearly for all those conveniences like front door ice and water.

I know people with big, power guzzling freezers with food in there left from the Thanksgiving meal back when uncle Henry was twenty years younger. Those things use a lot of power to freeze food you may never eat or even forget is in there. If you plan to freeze a side of beef, think about how much fresh beef you can buy compared with the cost of freezing it. The store keeps it cold until you need it.

When the power is off, you could lose money by stocking up on a six-month supply of meat, etc. Use the refrigerator freezer for meat storage if you must. Keep bread in a plastic box to keep it fresh. Putting bread in the refrigerator also helps. With planning, you can have a more efficient kitchen, spend less time in it, and save money at the same time.

WHEN SHOULD I NOT PAY OFF A DEBT?

Americans are struggling under near-record debt loads today. Less equity in our homes and bigger credit card balances add to the burden. Bankruptcies are at new highs, and foreclosures are setting records. With these problems, should you really pay off debt?

How do you know which debt to pay off first? Many people say they should pay down their home mortgages. Many are paying extra monthly in addition to the regular payments. Some even try to get 15-year loans, compared to 30-year loans.

While Americans are trying to rid themselves of debt, they ignore other debts and obligations that will eventually cost them more. It makes no sense to speed up paying off low-interest debts that are tax deductible if you carry other debts such as credit cards, car loans, personal loans, etc. Your first goal should be to pay off the highest interest debt, one that is not tax deductible. Pay off the credit cards, personal loans and car loans first before considering paying off a deductible student loan or home mortgage. Mortgage interest is the last debt you want to pay as long as you owe high-interest accounts.

Paying off certain debts is not a good idea when you are neglecting your retirement savings. If your employer matches half of your 401k contribution up to 6% of your earnings, you're missing out on free employer money and the interest it will earn. Worse is the fact that this money and your missing contribution can't grow tax-deferred over the next thirty years. At an average 8% annual return, one year's contribution could have grown to more than $35,000.

If you're paying off debt with money you could be putting into your savings or retirement plan, you're saving a little and losing a lot. If the debt to be paid off is at a higher interest % than your savings %, it's correct to pay off that debt. Use low-interest money to pay off higher interest debt.

Consider a person with $250 extra a month trying to decide if he should pay off the car loan or fund a Roth IRA. If he pays the $250 as extra payments on a $20,000, five-year loan, he could be done in just under three years, at an interest savings of more than $1000. In those three years, he would have forever missed the chance to contribute the maximum annually into a Roth IRA. Those contributions could grow to nearly $78,000 in thirty years.

People still try to concoct schemes to tap into an IRA or 401K to pay off car loans, credit card balances or even mortgages. This borders insanity. Almost nobody will know how much money they'll lose to taxes and penalties when they withdraw the money. It may be as much as one fourth to one half of whatever is withdrawn, depending on state and federal tax brackets.

Once the money is withdrawn from a retirement plan, you can't put it back, and you've lost all that future tax-deferred compounded money. It makes you wonder how many people use 401K loans to avoid their real problem, overspending. If you borrow from your 401K and lose your job, you have to pay back the loan in short order, or it will be taxed and penalized as a distribution

I've seen people who pay off bills in short periods of time. I've also seen people who struggle with their bills and simply can't pay them off. They borrow from their invest-ment funds, tap home equity and struggle to pay medical bills or credit card bills. These people have no hope of financial recovery. Some lose their jobs, divorce, etc., while others stupidly fail due to greed or bungling. Some blame belongs to financial institutions that keep giving credit to people who can't handle it.

Bankruptcy is there for a reason. It gives people a new start and protects their homes, etc. so they can possibly recover from their mistakes. It's not the perfect solution, but it can be the best of some very bad decisions made through life. Bankruptcy lawyers try to convince you to let them file for you, while credit counselors are in the business of getting you to pay off your debts.

The National Foundation for Consumer Credit says they actually turn away 3-10% of people who ask for counseling to pay off debts because these people are too far in debt to repay their bills in the 3-5 year guideline the foundation requires. If a credit counselor tells you they can't help you, it's probably time to file.

WHAT IS YOUR DEBT REDUCTION PLAN?

Do you have a debt reduction plan? If not, you're already in trouble. You must set a plan to get out of debt. If you're floating down the middle of a river and never make an effort to reach the bank, you'll never get out of the river.

Americans are swimming in debt, almost $7 billion worth of it. It's like paying for dinners again and again after you've eaten, like still paying for clothing you've worn and disposed of. The memories are gone, but the debt remains, a monthly reminder that I'm shortsighted and materialistic.

Don't carry several credit cards, with balances on all of them. Identify the card with the highest interest rate, and pay it off as soon as possible. Then do the same with the others. Then throw all but one of them away. Don't let the monthly balance go over to the next month. Pay the balance. If you don't think you can do this, throw that one away, too.

You'll feel great when one debt is fully paid off. The next one will make you jump with joy. The momentum will feed itself to get us out of debt totally. The average American household with at least one credit card carries an average of $8000 in debt. Decide to quit charging on the card, then pay all possible monthly until the thing is history. Look at the balance and determine how many months you want to take to pay it off. Don't blink. Just do it. That $8000 balance would require a $444 payment monthly for 18 months to pay off. Debt is like being in quicksand. You struggle and complain, but it won't let you go. You must break free or avoid the quicksand completely. It won't be as easy as it was when Silver used a rope to pull the Lone Ranger from it, but you can do it if you dedicate yourself to it.

Talking about getting out of debt won't work unless you put your doing where your mouth is. You must spend less than you bring home. Start now. If you don't have money to buy it, don't buy it. Don't plan on making more money later. Do it now.

Look at your cable bill. Do you have too many extras? Give up the cell phone. Do you really need to do all that talking outside the home? If so, maybe you should keep the cell phone and give up the service phone in the house. Bring lunch to work. Avoid sub-scribing to magazines, television program guides or even newspapers. These aren't big savers, but they add up. By the way, all those cable channels are unnoticed when you're down to educational and fix-it stations.

Call the credit card company and tell them you are planning to move the balance to another card. Ask them is they'll cut the interest rate if you stay with them. They do have the authority to cut the rate. Then, call back a month later and try it again.

Debt consolidation is very tricky. To put all card balances onto one card at a low rate may look great, but you should ask about hidden fees and how long that low rate will be honored. If you consolidate correctly, you may reduce membership fees and late pay-ments. Start paying and quit spending.

You alone got yourself into your financial mess. Learn to get out of it and to stay out of it. The challenge will teach you a lot about money and lead to a happier life for you and yours.

Once you've gotten the upper hand on your finances, try to help a friend. Share with them how you did it, or tell them where they can get a copy of this book. You can't imagine the gratification you get from helping others.

REPEAT AFFIRMATIONS UNTIL THEY ARE FACTS.

Affirmations are positive statements of fact as you intend them to be. Because the affirmations are "statements of fact", they must be written in the present tense—the sub-conscious can only operate in the present, never in the future. Affirmations must be re-peated over and over until they are facts.

"If I can't afford to pay cash for it, I can't afford it". "I am free of debt". "I operate on a cash-only basis". These can be your affirmations.

Negative affirmations are more common than positive ones. You've said many times, "This will never work". Then when it didn't work, you said, "See, I told you". The point has now become a fact. Hate and prejudice are great examples of negative affirmation.

What we're taught as children stays with us throughout our lives. Elephants are tied with light chains when they could easily break free. Why? It's simple. When they were babies, they had a heavy chain on their foot from which they couldn't break loose. As they grew older, they didn't forget. This is strange, but it's how we live.

We continue to put limits on ourselves. We have no idea what we can accomplish. Buddist monks can control their heartbeat and blood pressure with their minds. They can also dry a wet sheet placed around their bodies using their body heat, which they also regulate. Our minds can limit us to things we truly believe we can't do. What does this have to do with overspending/saving? Our minds have to be programmed to do either and can be reprogrammed with work and patience.

A barracuda is separated in a tank of water from minnows by a sheet of clear plastic. The big barracuda continues to bump into the plastic when trying to get to the minnows. After a period of time, the plastic sheet is removed, and the barracuda will not try to get to the minnows because he was taught he can't go through the plastic sheet. We have invisible barriers separating us from things we can do, but think we cannot do. Do we rule our minds, or do our minds rule us?

How many times does an affirmation have to be repeated? It takes as many times as it takes to get the job done. It doesn't matter if it's important enough. If it's not important enough, why are you considering it?

Try these. Repeat them over and over or simply read them every day.
I'll buy a repair manual and do my own repairs.
I will contribute to a retirement plan either at work or at a bank.
I will buy a home.
I'll buy only what I need.
I will set up automatic deposit to a savings account from my paycheck.
I will buy generic and store-brand goods and household products.
I will not buy, but rent things I only occasionally use.
I will pay extra on my mortgage each month.
I will not purchase a new car before mine has 60,000 miles on it.
I will not loan money to friends.
I will not expect social security to be enough to live on after retirement.
I will try to use CD's instead of low-interest savings accounts.
I will spend less on Christmas.
I will take a course that offers instructions on how to make money and save some.
I will grocery shop with a list.
I will not take anyone grocery shopping with me.
I will not invest money in things I don't understand.
I will buy life insurance for the kids while it is cheap.
I will now buy things just because they're on sale.
I will reduce or quit my buying from television home shopping shows.
I will not buy lottery tickets on a regular basis.

BUT I'M TOO OLD TO GET AN ALLOWANCE.

Most of us got an allowance as a child. Mine helped buy gas for the car I borrowed from my dad. Then, we didn't have our own cars. I didn't get paid for doing the chores. We were expected to do those anyway.

Come kids spent their allowance within hours of the time they received it. Others saved it for something special, like a baseball or some sort of game to play. As adults, we earn a paycheck from our employer. Let's think about this allowance thing.

Try giving yourself an allowance. I know. You say you can't afford to do this. Just try it. You may have to give up some of the things you spent money on before. Simply take $5, $10 or $20 from your paycheck and consider it as an allowance to do with what you please. Now, ask yourself what you want to do with it. Immediately, you get the feeling you have been given a bonus. You won't miss it from your paycheck.

This is one of the easiest ways to make an affirmation that you'll save some money, either in a sock drawer, in the back of your wallet, or in a savings account. You can actually do this without really seeing the money. Just go to a bank or credit union and ask them to have your employer automatically deposit a certain amount to a Christmas club or other savings account. Even if you just put $50 a month or $12 a week into such an account, you'll get a surprise after a year when your account is worth more than $600, enough to cover Christmas expenses, property taxes or even to leave it to earn more money. The bigger the account gets, the better you'll feel. Your allowance has been well spent.

I have grandchildren who are totally different when it comes to money. One will save all or most of an allowance, while the other will rush out and spend it as soon as possible. As adults, we're not so different than kids. Some of us can't wait to get that big IRS re-fund check back, money you have loaned the government for a year interest free, to go out and buy something you would not have bought if you had not gotten a refund. Money can do strange, great and devastating things to us.

Giving yourself an allowance will let you throw change into a jar, money in the rat hole in your wallet or into an account to grow larger. Which will you do? We must learn, unlearn and relearn throughout our lives. We learn as a child. We unlearn to re-program ourselves to do things better or differently. We relearn by convincing ourselves that what we learned in the past doesn't necessarily work today. Things have changed. That doesn't mean we should go out and spend, spend and spend. It means we now must take a more concentrated effort not to be sucked into the spending habits we're bomb-barded with on television, radio and other means of communications.

Don't wait. Start now giving yourself an allowance. This simple tool will teach you to save and spend wisely. We need a gimmick today to help us know the value of money. A dollar today is still worth as much as a dollar long ago. It's the way we use the dollar that makes it equal to, less than or the same as before.

As you see your savings from your allowance grow, you'll be less tempted to spend it. If you are always short on money when the wedding anniversary or the spouse's birthday comes around, reach into your saved allowance and redeem yourself.

My dad used to put dollar bills in his safe deposit box on a regular basis. It wasn't a lot of money, but he looked at the pile of money as if it was a fortune. You'll feel the same way when your allowance builds into a nest egg.

DID MONEY BURN THAT HOLE IN YOUR POCKET?

We've all heard the expression that money is burning a hole in our pocket. Just exactly what does that mean? It means the money wants to get out of our pocket so it can be spent and go into another person's pocket. We all keep change in our front pockets or purses, paper money in our wallets or purse. Why do we carry this money on our person? It's in case we see something we want or we just simply know we're making plans to spend that money today. If you left most of this money at home, would it change your spending habits? It probably would. We carry change in the coin holders in our cars. That's just in case the bill is more than paper money by a few cents. Some people pay a $2.31 bill with a $20 bill instead of a $5 bill just so it will seem like they have more money in their pockets.

If the money is really burning a hole in our pocket, how do we control it and contain it? We simply don't keep as much of it in our pockets, or we occasionally put our hand in our pocket and feel the money, knowing it's still there. You must understand that money doesn't literally want to get out of our pocket and be spent. It feels warm and happy in there. It's you who awakens it and gives it to someone else. The only burning is that burning desire within us to spend, spend and spend. We act like all that money in our pocket is extra money to do with what we please. It's actually the same money you got when you cashed your check. Some of it went to your checking account, some on cash-paid bills, the balance into your own little vault, your pocket.

Have you ever felt the money in your pocket and tried to guess how much it amounted to or what the coins were. Sure you have. Then you take it out and see if you were right. That money in your pocket is yours until you give it to someone else for goods or services. The moment you do this, it's not yours anymore. It's in somebody else's pocket to burn a hole in it. Have you ever thought of the cycle money must take in a short period of time? In one day, money spent at a flea market may go into and out of many pockets, and every time it did, it was spent over and over again.

I always carry enough money in my pocket to give a tip after a meal. The balance is put into jars, to be saved, rolled and deposited. Coins are money, too.

While in Germany years ago, I had about five different types of change from different countries in my pocket. In Amsterdam, I spent paper money, not knowing some of the coins are worth more. I had no idea how much money I had on me. When you consider five different types of coins, paper money from at least six countries, my credit card and traveler's checks, it wasn't easy keeping up with it.

Money doesn't have anything to do with the size of it. All paper money is the same size, a dime smaller than a nickel, and a penny just larger than a dime. It's the value of the money that counts.

When you feel money burning a hole in your pocket, pet it and keep it around. You'll both be happier. Your money doesn't ask to be spent. It's your willingness to spend it that brings it out of your pocket.

All pockets need zippers on them or a button to make it harder to get to the money. If we would train ourselves to just walk away when we see something we just have to have, we'd be amazed at how much we would have spent.

Money is simply a tool with which to get through life. Be good to it, and make it your long-time companion.

YOU AIN'T GOT NO MONEY. YOU JUST AIN'T NO GOOD.

We've all heard the Ray Charles classic, "Hit the road, Jack". In this song, the girl singer tells Ray, "You ain't got no money. You just ain't no good".

Does having or not having money make you good or bad? I guess if you're looking for a gold-digger or just a lonely girl looking for security, it does. The truth is that it's the people who look like they don't have money who do have it. Others are in debt up to their eyeballs and want the world to look at them as being successful or something.

As a teenager, we'd ask a girl for a date. That was back when a date was actually planned in advance and was a special occasion. She never cared or asked how much money we had. We probably had a maximum of $5 on us at any one time. Of course, to take her to a movie, buy her popcorn and a coke and ride her around town to let our buddies gaze upon her cost only about $4 then. Things have changed, haven't they?

I used to have an allowance, all $5 of it, changed to $1 bills to look like I had a lot of money. If we really wanted to impress our dates, we'd roll up the money and keep it in our pocket. Then we'd whip out our bankroll, flip off the dollars and quickly put the rest back into our pocket.

Does it really take a lot of money to have friends? They are probably as near broke as you are. Money goes right up there with hair, a tight abdomen, tanned skin, etc. as the things most people think is necessary to get chicks, impress the wife or girlfriend or impress their buddies. We must not get caught in the trap of thinking money is a status symbol. If you're carrying around a lot of cash, it's probably because you forgot to pay some of the bills. Money is used for that, you know, paying bills.

Another trick used to be to put a $5 bill on top of a few $1 bills and make everyone think you had a stack of fives. You have only what you have.

If your bills are paid up, and you have a few bucks left, you're better off than the guy with a roll of cash that was supposed to be paid on his power bill. I was taught at a young age to pay bills first, even if nothing is left. You just go by the best you could. To go out on a spending spree with a credit card just because you don't have money isn't the way to get ahead. When your bills are paid and you have little or nothing left, sit and watch your favorite show on television. After all, you have paid the cable bill.

If you carry a lot of cash to make you feel good, think of why you're doing it in the first place. Is it to impress someone, so you can buy whatever you want or simply that you just feel more secure?

I know people who don't have a checking account or a savings account. One guy had one of those little coin holders that opened up when squeezed. I played golf with him once, and he lost it during the match. He said he had some $100 bills in it and needed it to pay monthly bills. I asked him why he kept money that way without using a bank. He said he didn't trust banks. That's strange, huh?

So, if your bills are paid and you have $6 left in your pocket, smile and think of those people you meet who carry large amounts of cash on them, but leave their bills unpaid. You're a lot better off than they are.

WHAT DOES "SPEND" AND "SAVE" MEAN?

All of us spend. We all save either to spend later or to hold onto it. Do you really know what spend and save mean? Lets take a little walk through the world of spend and save.

The definition of spend is: to use up or pay out—to wear out or exhaust—to consume wastefully—to squander—to cause or permit to elapse—to give up or sacrifice—to expend or waste wealth—to become expended or consumed.

Let's break up the definitions and take a good look at what spending really is. We use the money to pay it out to someone for goods or services. When we've spent all we have, we have exhausted our money fund. We all know what consuming wastefully is. We've either done it or will do it at some time in our lives. Some people do it more than others. If we spend wastefully, we either buy things we don't need or we pay too much for what we buy. Of course, we have to do our homework to know if prices are too high. To squander would be like betting your last $50 on one roll of the dice. To sacrifice sounds like doing without and not spending, but we sacrifice the hard work we've done to earn the money when we spend it in a wasteful manner. You may think you aren't wealthy, but if you have $100 and the other guy has $0, you're wealthy in his eyes. To be wealthy is different for most people. Some think $1 million makes you wealthy. But if you go out and spend it all on a pleasure boat, you aren't wealthy anymore. Your money is consumed when you spend it. Then the person to whom you gave the money can save it or spend it as you have done.

I've heard of spendable income. Isn't all money spendable? Sure it is, but it's your decision to either spend or save it. Some say spendable money is what they have on them at the time. My dad used to carry several hundred dollars on him most of the time. He'd borrow the money from the bank each year, carry it around, then pay it back with interest at the end of the year. I guess the temptation of breaking a $100 bill wasn't as great as breaking a $10 bill. He just felt secure knowing he had all that money on him.

The phrase "pocket money" is just what it says, pocket money. To me, pocket money is a small amount of paper money and change for tips. I use my credit card for almost everything. Then, I pay the balance each month. I've borrowed money for one-month interest free by doing this. Pocket money is for unexpected expenses, small ones. I've seen people who carry a roll of money in their pocket. What a way to lose it, get robbed or simply spend more. Banks are for holding money. That's where most of your money belongs.

A "spend thrift" is one who spends improvidently or wastefully. Ask yourself if you're a spend thrift. Your answer may surprise you. If you spend $6 a day to go out to lunch, you're a spend thrift. If you use 93 octane gasoline instead of the 87 octane your manual suggests, you're a spend thrift. If you buy soda drinks from a vending machine when traveling instead of carrying a small six-pack cooler, you're a spend thrift. You see, you don't have to buy $50,000 cars or $500,000 homes to be a spend thrift. All those small wasteful expenditures add up to making you a spend thrift.

Now that we've explored the meaning of "spend", let's look at the word "save". We've all saved something in our lives. We've saved that hat we like to wear, that pair of boots we've depended on throughout thick and thin, or that piggy bank full of change for a rainy day.

The word "save" means: to put by as a store or reserve—accumulate—to keep from being lost to an opponent—to prevent an opponent from scoring or winning—to avoid unnecessary waste or expense.

Now let's explore the word "save". To put a reserve means to put it away for a later time. To accumulate, you have to make it more or bigger in time. This means you must be serious about saving. Set a goal to save a predetermined amount of money. To keep money from being lost to an opponent requires determination and dedication on your part. The opponent is the person who desperately wants you to spend your money on his goods or services. When you do so, you've let him win. That money will never come back to your reserve. The opponent will simply spend it for other goods or services. It's like a viscous cycle of spending. Your part is to win the game by spending less than you bring home. Leave it up to others to make the opponent rich. It takes a lot of will power to resist giving money away. We all need to avoid the unnecessary waste or expense. If our parents didn't train us to do this, we must train ourselves or get help from those who know how to help us.

Don't be ashamed to admit your inability to handle money. The sooner you get help or simply change your spending and savings habits, the sooner you'll see your way clear and begin to see that you haven't worked hard to waste it.

Unlike the government, you can't simply crank up the presses and create more money. You must earn money and somehow spend less than you earn. You would think the government would learn to do this too, wouldn't you?

BUT IT'S A BARGAIN, ISN'T IT?

Just what is a bargain? It's different to almost everyone. It may mean saving ten cents on a hamburger. It may be saving $80 on a refrigerator or ten cents on a gallon of gasoline.

Let's look into the word and see what it really means. Bargain means: advantageous purchase-negotiate over the terms of a purchase, agreement or contract- to haggle-to come to term-to sell or dispose of by bargaining-barter.

When is a purchase advantageous? To whom is it advantageous? If you pay $10 less than the price tag on an item, it doesn't mean you've received a bargain. If you bought a new car from under a large tent in front of the dealership instead of from the lot or show room, does it mean you got a bargain? If you've done your homework to find out how different prices are for an item, then negotiate for it, you've probably gotten a bargain. If you're one of those people who don't like to haggle for the purchase of what you want, you seldom get a bargain.

My uncle is the world's most experienced haggler. I once saw him haggle with a gas station employee over the price of a quart of kerosene. He haggled for ten minutes and saved a dime. He left the station feeling he had gotten a bargain. His answer was always that time spent haggling is time well spent. I once purchased a sofa from a major chain store. I haggled with the salesman even though he continued to say they couldn't discount the price of the sofa. When he tried to charge me a carrying charge, I told him I had my truck outside, that I'd carry it myself. He did get me some help to carry it from the store to my truck.

Most people don't know what bartering is. To barter is to trade or exchange by or as if by bartering. If you trade eggs for milk, your yard work for food or your professional services for a golf game, you're bartering. My wife and I have attended as vendors at craft sales for years. On the last day, I'd always wait until an hour or so before the end of the sale, then walk around to the other crafters and ask if they'd like to barter. Some of them looked at me like they wanted to call the police or get up and slap me. Others knew what I meant. Our craft items cost about $.30 each to make, and we sold them for $1.00 each. I'd barter with the vendors for their craft items. Once, I asked a lady who had beautiful large dolls for sale for $40 each if she'd like to barter for some of my craft items. She traded me a $40 doll for 40 of my items. This meant I had spent $12 to make them and had actually received a doll that would have cost $40. My granddaughter enjoyed the doll, and I saved at least $28 on the deal. It works. Try it. You can even buy things at a flea market and walk around and barter for something you need.

You've seen the commercials that say you can buy one pair of shoes for $20 and get a second pair free. You immediately think of the shoes as $10 a pair. Ask the question if you really needed an extra pair of shoes. If you do, do you need tow new pairs? Do you really think a bargain is buying ten mailboxes just because they're on sale for 70% off?

I'M NOT BROKE. I'VE GOT $500 IN THE BANK.

Ask ten people what being financially broke means. You'll get ten different answers. Your answer will probably be different, too.

A survey shows 60% of people who retire will have $0 in the bank, $0 investment income and will still owe such bills as cars, houses, etc. That is an awful thought. Since your social security payments are based on your income, you'll draw considerably less social security than if you were still drawing a paycheck.

People who have $500 in the bank think they're okay financially. Let's think about that. If your total monthly expenses are $1600, you have 31% of a month's bills in the bank. That means you have enough money to live for 9.5 days. If you can't add to that $500 monthly and leave it alone, you're technically broke.

If your family is like the average American family and your monthly bills amount to $2400, you have only 6.4 days of bill money. That's less than a week. Of course, many, many people have the $2400 monthly bills and have no checking account, no savings account, no 401K, etc. You are the working poor. The only difference in you and someone with no paycheck and no home is that you could lose your home and your paycheck any time. You must realize your situation and do whatever is necessary to turn it around.

If you have determined you are in serious financial trouble, start by reducing your spending. Then, get a part time job for a few hours a week to increase your bank account. With the extra money from the part time job and the reduced spending, you'll see an immediate change in your financial situation. Then, don't slide back into your old habits.

If you don't have a checking account, you're spending too much money out of your pocket. It's better to write a check than to carry lots of money with you, which will tempt you to spend more on things you don't need. If your checking account balance isn't above the limit to prevent your paying a fee for a low balance, fix it as soon as possible. The more your balance shows, the less you'll want to spend.

When you get more than four months bill money in your bank account, put part of it into a CD and earn interest on it. Then build the balance back up again and create another CD. It's fun to do this. It is a great way to save.

If you think having $500 in the bank puts you on easy street, you may just be close to being put out on the street. If you're 30 years old and have worked for 10 years, you've probably earned about $200,000. The $500 nest egg now amounts to only one quarter of one percent of what you've earned. That means you've wasted a lot of money somewhere.

Do whatever it takes to increase your bank account, and if it means paying high interest credit cards off early to get it done, do it. If it means you can't rent $30 worth of movie videos weekly, then do it. You'll be proud of yourself.

SEND ME $10, AND I'LL TELL YOU HOW TO GET RICH.

You've all seen the ads that tell you that you can get rich quick. Believe me, the only way to get rich quickly is to inherit it from uncle Johnny or win the lottery. It takes time and patience and hard work to make money.

I saw an ad that stated if you'd send the person $10, he'd tell you how to get rich like he did. Later, I read that this guy had legally cheated thousands of people out of their $10. What he did was very simple. You send him $10 and he sends you a letter telling you to run an ad for people to send you $10, and you would send them the same letter telling them to do the same thing. This wasn't illegal. He plainly stated his intention to tell you how to get rich. I'm sure it made some people richer than others. Others simply lost $10.

It costs a fair amount of money for people to run this type of ad, and they run them every week for years. Can you imaging how much money they're getting from people who fall for these ideas?

Unless you're a crook, inherit a lot of money, or win the lottery, the way to wealth is to work for many years and know how to handle money.

Stop and think of the ways some people rip us off for money. The check-cashing companies are making tons of money cashing checks for a small fee. When I was a kid, back in the 50's, a guy used to stand on the corner in front of the cotton mill in which my parents worked. He held a large tray of money. People in the mill probably took home about $28 a week. For $.25, the guy would cash their checks for them. As I played in the park close by, I wondered how he could make much money doing this. Then I calculated that if he cashed 100 checks a week, he had made the same amount of money one of the mill workers took home

85

in a week. And it took him an hour a week to do this. He worked for a furniture company full time.

You've all seen those car title-pawn-shops that have open up all over the country. Have you ever wondered why there are so many cars parked around those shops? It's true that you get to keep the car, but they get the title; and if you can't pay them back the money you borrowed, you lose the car. What would bring any person to the point to borrow a few hundred dollars and pawn your title? How did they get to that point? That's like being thrown overboard 100 miles out in the ocean and trying to swim to shore. You're not going to make it. If you're in that financial condition, go home, sit down, get a pen and pad; and start writing down how you'll turn the situation around.

I knew a guy who loaned money for a living. The interest rate was about 25%, and he'd never loan over $500 to anyone. Some people would borrow $100 from him and pay back most of it, and borrow more. They were in debt so far they couldn't pay him back. If you find yourself in the situation that a couple of hundred dollars stands between you and being broke, you are broke already. The only way out is not through a loan shark or even leaning on uncle Johnny. It's by thinking of how you got into that situation, then planning on how to get out of it.

Don't fall for get-rich-quick schemes. They only make the schemer richer, not you. The next time you're tempted to go for one of them, turn and walk away. Use your brain to find your way out. That's what the schemer did.

CUT IT IN HALF TO SAVE MONEY.

When trying to save money in the home, a lot of things can be cut in half or just used as half measure. Lots of things do just as well when using half of them.

Try using half of the dryer softener sheet, half the recommended amount of detergent, half a cotton ball, etc. It really works and saves you money. Buy instant drink mixes without sugar, then use half the amount of sugar normally used. Your children don't need all that sugar, anyway.

Save lids from mayonnaise and coffee jars. When you have bacon drippings or oil from fried foods, pour it into the lids. When the lids are full, put the top back on the jar into the trash. This will prevent your drains from being clogged with oil and keep your garbage cans from getting so messy.

Save plastic milk containers and fill them with water and freeze them. Use them in camper coolers to keep drinks and food cold.

Leftover pancake batter makes food fried onion rings. Let the onion rings soak in the batter for twenty minutes. Then fry in hot oil.

Freeze coffee left over in ice cube trays. Then, when you want only a cup or so, pop the cubes into the microwave for a treat.

By using odd kitchen items, you can save on others. Put rice in a saltshaker to keep the salt from getting hard and clumpy. You can keep plastic wrap in the refrigerator to prevent it from sticking the next time you use it. You can reheat small portions of leftover food in the same pan by wrapping them individually in foil and placing in water covering the bottom of the pan. When you have a spill in the oven, sprinkle salt on it immediately. When the oven cools, wipe it off. Before pouring tomato-based sauces into Tupperware, spray the containers with nonstick cooking spray. You won't have stains. Save store-bought bread bags and ties to put homemade bread in.

To save on dishwasher cost, run it only when full. When adding dishes, take a hand-full of baking soda and sprinkle the dishes and bottom of the dishwasher to absorb odors. When you run the dishwasher, there is no need to add detergent to the first cycle, only to the second one. The baking soda will take the place of the detergent in the first cycle.

When converting your favorite recipe for microwave cooking, reduce the liquid by one fourth. Liquid does not evaporate in the microwave as much as in a conventional oven.

Before going on vacation, place a baggie with a few ice cubes in the freezer. If the power fails while you are gone and the food thaws and refreezes, you will know about it when you get home.

Transfer jelly into small plastic squeeze bottles. You don't have the sticky problem with jars, and you don't even have to use a knife. This works with homemade salad dressing, too.

So, cut down in the kitchen and save money. We're probably trained by the suppliers of the things we use to over-use, therefore buying more and more.

CUT HOUSEHOLD EXPENSES THE SIMPLE WAY.

You'd be amazed at how much money you spend on things around the house. We constantly upgrade, replace, fix and repair small things that we either must have or think we do.

If you have a problem with lint on your dark clothing, use a piece of nylon netting material to brush the line away. If you have trouble finding the end of a roll of tape the next time you use it, try this. Place a button or washer at the end each time you finish using the tape. You can easily find the end. You can even use tea as a permanent stain for unstained furniture.

When you empty your next jar of mayonnaise, clean and dry it, then sprat it with white paint inside. You can store valuables or even money in the refrigerator. Instead of buying an expensive can of bolt loosening material, simply wrap a cloth soaked in some carbonated water around the bolt. It should loosen after a short time.

Instead of making extra trips to the corner market for milk, buy more than one container and freeze it. When you've used half of one, take the frozen one out of the freezer and place it in the bottom of the refrigerator. Your freezer will run more efficiently if you have more food in it. So will your oven when you cook.

Instead of buying new scissors when they become dull, simply cut a few pieces of fine sandpaper with them to sharpen them. Place a metal spoon into a glass before you pour hot liquid into it. This will prevent the glass from cracking. If you have a problem with buttons coming off, place a small amount of nail polish to the thread on the face of the button. This will make it harder for the threads to break.

If you want to take food stains off your hands, use a slice of raw potato on it and wash your hands in cool water. Store brown sugar in the freezer to prevent it from hardening. A substitute for air freshener is to squeeze a few drops of lemon juice into the dust bag of your vacuum cleaner.

To save on heating and cooling, close off rooms you seldom use. You can even close the vents in these rooms to keep other rooms cooler or warmer. Use a paintbrush to do your dusting. It'll reach into hard to reach places. Use crumbled newspaper to clean your windows in the house and the car instead of expensive paper towels. Stock up with windshield washer fluid at an automotive store.

Use vegetable shortening to clean grease off your hands. Add vinegar to your dish-water to get grease off of dishes. You can also use it to clean furniture. Cut holes in the top of a jar lid and place baking soda in it. If you have grease on wallpaper, apply baby powder to a powder puff. Rub the spot and watch it disappear.

Household ammonia will clean a paint brush. An eraser will remove heel marks from your floor. You can rub a white candle into each corner of your window sills to keep them free of moisture and dust. You can remove small scratches from polished furniture by rubbing them with a shell from a walnut. Silver jewelry won't oxidize if you keep it in a zip lock bag.

Clean rings around your tub or shower with toothpaste and an old tooth brush. Clean inside of glass containers with lemon juice and salt. To clean carpet, use another piece of carpet. Reuse zip-lock bags by washing them and storing them in the freezer.

Save those happy meal boxes. Then, simply fill them with other types of foods for the child. You can also put novelty items like pencils or small toys in them. Use the card-board egg cartons to start seed prior to outside planting.

Don't buy new candles. Melt down the old ones to make new ones. Broken crayons can be added for color. When dusting, use dryer softener sheets. They're also handy to remove soap scum from doors on the shower. Use old pillow cases for laundry bags. Don't throw away old clothing. Use them to make quilts, or give to someone who will make them if you're not.

Save a few old newspapers for starting small fires outside or as mulch for the garden. Store them in a grocery bag. The little plastic film holders can be used to hold buttons, nails and other small objects. Pantyhose can be used to buff your shoes or even secure plants in the garden.

Save gallon jugs to freeze water in to put in coolers for that day at the lake or just out riding around. You can also use the jugs after tops are cut out for potting plants. When unwrapping a bar of soap, put the wrapper in your linen closet for a fresh smell.

Pill bottles can be used for a variety of things. You can put pins, vitamins, coins, etc. in them, as well as nuts and bolts. If you have a small paper shredder, shred junk mail and use it for packaging material when shipping gifts to friends and family.

You can add salt to cold water to wash dark clothing for the first time to set the color. The same clothing can be kept bright by repeating this from time to time. Instead of spending on a dry cleaner, use Woolite or similar product to hand wash garments labeled "dry clean only". Always use warm or cold settings on your washing machine to wash. Then use cold water to rinse. You may save $100 a year by washing in cold water.

AT times, your washer needs washing, too. Run it on hot water and add a bottle of vinegar to clean the film of soap and scum that has built up inside the machine. You can avoid fading of your clothing by washing and drying them inside out. Tie socks together before washing so you can easily sort them later. Remember to clean the lint trap in the dryer "every" time you do laundry. You can actually make your own spray starch by mixing 2 tablespoons of cornstarch and 1 pint of cold water. Be sure to put it into a spray bottle and shake before each use.

I know some of these things sound trivial. Take my word for it. Each little trick you can use in the house will add up and save you big bucks. Share them with friends and family members. Everyone should know how to do things easier and cheaper.

We've been programmed to spend money on all sorts of things just because they're advertised to do certain things. Experiment a little, and learn lessons you can pass on to your children. They're going to need all the help they can get.

USE YOUR BRAIN, NOT THE LIFE'S SAVINGS, WHEN SHOPPING.

A little planning and thinking can save you plenty if you'll do it prior to shopping, not after. You need to have a plan. If you don't know what you're going to buy, you didn't need to go anyway.

Before starting out, look in your pantry and closets to see what you have. Don't spend money on things you don't need. Prepare a menu for the week around what you have. Then see what is on sale. If you know of a good co-op in your area, join now. Your weekly food bill could be cut by as much as one half. Don't run out of anything. If you do, you can't wait for sales.

Shop at larger stores, not smaller ones. The larger ones usually charge less for items. Unless it is absolutely necessary, don't ever go to the little store around the corner. You'll pay too much every time. Don't shop on an empty stomach. It's true you'll buy less if you aren't hungry. We eat at a restaurant across the street from the grocery store.

While shopping, stick to the things on your list to buy. Protein is necessary, but you can get it from many foods other than meat. Peanut butter, eggs, poultry, beans and cheese are less expensive and offer an excellent source of protein.

Buying whole chickens is cheaper than breasts only, unless you or yours are those who never had to eat necks and gizzards when a child. You can find the real bargains on the lower and higher shelves. The store personnel put the most expensive items at eye level. Believe me, they have meetings and plan this type of stuff. Try to have enough on hand to last until it is on sale.

Your freezer can help you save money. Buy multiples of things that are on sale. Freeze such things as cheese, milk and butter. Buy in bulk when possible. Look at prices. Larger sizes will not always be lower in price.

Many of you look at the packaging and may decide to buy because of it. Pretty packaging costs plenty. You're paying for the advertising and the packaging. Always check the dates of expiration on dairy products. Look at those items pushed back into the shelves or trays to find the freshest items.

Those wonderful convenience foods are more expensive. If you want to trade money for time, it's for you. If not, plan to prepare from non-convenience foods. With a little practice, you can learn the sales cycles of the stores. Then you can plan for these buys and put them on the list.

If you have a bakery close to home, use it. Rolls and bread can be bought in bulk and frozen for later use. No one store will have the best prices on all items. You may have to go to two or more stores to realize a total savings.

Sit down and plan to save money. Grocery shopping is no different than shopping for a car, furniture, etc. It's just on a smaller scale, but equally as important. If you can save enough in a year on groceries to pay one car payment, it's worth it. You can save a lot of money with a little patience and planning. Give it a try, and teach it to your kids.

HOW MUCH ENERGY CAN YOU AFFORD?

We all have the energy to get up in the morning and get to work so we can pay those dreaded home energy bills. Most of us can't control our paychecks, but we can control the amount of energy we use to heat and cool our homes.

I've lived at my present location for about twenty years. My home is brick. Since moving in, I've had all exposed wood on the exterior covered with vinyl and aluminum. I've gone from a large power guzzling electric furnace to propane heat. I've gone to energy-efficient appliances. I've gone to 15-watt fluorescent bulbs putting out the same light as a regular 60-watt bulb. They last for years, too. I've installed double pane windows and performed other energy savings attempts to keep the costs down.

You don't have to install new windows or more efficient appliances to save money, though. The home improver's lament is: You can't afford to. You can't afford not to.

It's understandable that many homeowners don't have the cash to spend on the expense required to begin seeing a pay-off. But you can do several things to reduce those fat utility bills.

Buy a programmable thermostat. They cost about $30, and most people can install them. If nobody is home during the day or night, these thermostats are great. They can be set to turn on a half hour before you get home so you haven't wasted all that energy while at work. Maybe you want to control the air or heat while asleep. Simply set the thermostat to turn on before you get up in the morning.

I know it's a messy job, but installing or adding more energy-efficient insulation in your attic can really reduce those energy bills. Almost anyone can roll out this product, and it doesn't take a long time to install. This is a one-shot deal, and you'll be glad you took the time to install it.

Caulking around windows and weather-stripping at drafty doors is an immediate payback. It is stated that a quarter inch gap at the bottom of a standard door can equal the energy loss of a three-inch by three-inch hole in the wall. This is a job you can do your-self. Just take a little time, and you'll be proud of yourself.

Lighting can be a substantial energy drain. Most people don't know the cost of lighting. Let's look into this. If you use 100-watt bulbs and have four bulbs in your overhead fixture, you can easily calculate the weekly, monthly or annual cost of lighting. Ask your power company what the kilowatt rate cost is in your area. Assume \$.07 per kilowatt. A kilowatt is 1000 watts. If you use four bulbs, you're using 400-killowatts every hour. It takes 2.5 hours to use a kilowatt or \$.07 for the cost of lighting. If you use this fixture ten hours a day, your monthly lighting cost will be about \$8.40 for that one fixture. If you have eight lights on, your monthly cost will increase to \$16.80. That's a sizeable piece of your total monthly power bill.

Compact fluorescent bulbs are much more energy-efficient than standard bulbs, and they'll last for years instead of weeks or months. Sure they cost more initially, but the payback is obvious. They consume little power and generate very little heat, another savings by not having to cool the area due to bulb heat.

If you can possible afford Energy Star appliances or windows, go for it. The windows are said to save as much as 15% of a home's heating bill. They're twice as efficient as windows made just a few years ago. They're thicker and block out sound, too. It's true that replacing windows can cost thousands of dollars. Look at the length of time you'll be in the home, though.

There is another energy efficient way to save money, too. It's canned Energy Efficient Mortgage. This little known mortgage is federally recognized, available in all fifty states, and can be applied to most home mortgages. The fact that energy saving homeowners will have lower utility bills and more cash left over, they can afford larger mortgages and have a more marketable home. A new Fannie Mae energy mortgage program allows you to borrow up to 15% more than the value of the home with no additional down payment.

You must first have a Home Energy Ratings System efficiency inspector probe the place and establish an energy rating. Factors such as appliance efficiency, types of windows, utility rates and insulation are considered. The rating is given between 1 and 100, with 100 being the highest efficiency rating. Take this information to a lender and ask for an energy mortgage. If the lender doesn't seem familiar with this type program, bring it to their attention.

Horizontal access washing machines, like used widely in Europe, use 30 to 40% less energy and much less water than conventional units. They fill from the bottom and don't require the entire machine to be filled to wash.

Maybe the government will give tax incentives for energy efficient installations for residential and commercial construction. Don't hold your breath, but it could happen.

YOU CAN BUILD A HOME WITHOUT GOING TO THE POORHOUSE.

We've all heard the horror stories about big construction projects cost running much more than budgeted. It happens when building a residential home, too.

Building a home is like buying a car in the sense that you want to keep piling on accessories. Location and square footage are the main differences in home building. A home in Boston can cost 40% more than the same home in Atlanta.

The labor cost can vary widely from the northeast to the rural south. During a housing boom, the labor may be more, less if employment in the building trade is evident. Material costs can also vary, depending on the price of lumber, logging restrictions, and the distance the materials must be shipped.

Local government regulations can really affect building cost. The city council or design review committee can force you and/or your architect back for several visits. You need to find out if the environmental restrictions are strictly enforced. Some inner city districts abound with restrictions that will drive you crazy and will not make much sense at all.

The shape of your home can affect the price widely. You can have all sorts of weird angles and custom built items that really increase the total cost. You can have one or six bathrooms, or can pay $25 or $1000 for a faucet. Sit down ant think of what you will really need. If you have no kids, plan for later. If you're at the age of being kid-free, you'll want to scale back.

If you have a construction loan, the lender will insist that you have a budget. Architects will be costly, but they can save you substantial money, too. If you don't use an architect, get bids from at least three builders. Have a good idea of how much you can afford, maybe one-fourth of your family take-home pay.

On a square footage basis, a larger home could be less costly than a smaller one due to the fact that the most costly parts, the kitchen, heating and cooling systems and plumbing are spread out over more footage. A two-story house can cost less than a one-story house of the same footage because the roof and foundation are smaller.

Most builders will tell you that your dream home will cost 10% more than you thought. If you are thousands of dollars short, where will you get the difference? Plan smartly, and don't build more home than you really need. The insurance, taxes and upkeep will be in proportion to the size of the home and how it is built.

So, you really can build a home without going to the poorhouse. Just use common sense and don't overspend to the point that your dream home becomes a disaster, a cause of divorce, or even worse, a trip to the poorhouse.

MONEY WILL DRIVE YOU CRAZY OR PUT YOU AT EASE.

Money is like water. You can't do without it. It causes more worry and brings more joy than we can comprehend. It is a tool of destruction or a resolution to all our problems.

How much time do you spend worrying about money and bills? It's quite a lot, I can assure you. Money seems to run our lives and ruin our lives. Money can be good or bad. Money is just an object that sits there until someone uses it for good or bad. It can pay hospital bills or drug bills. It can bring great joy or devastating problems.

If you truly want to streamline your financial life, you will need to take the time to establish a plan to do so. You, not your neighbors and friends, are responsible for your financial success or failure.

If you've ever bounced a check, it can be quite embarrassing and cost you money. Set up over-draft protection at your bank. It will come in a line of credit that comes in when you write a check for more than your balance. A small fee will be charged, and you'll have to pay interest charges on the amount charged to the line of credit. Don't abuse it. You still must control your check writing.

Use direct deposit to save time at the bank or trips to the bank. It's said that one third of those working don't use this service. Go to your payroll office and inquire about it. It's easy, and you won't get your hands on al that money to be tempted to spend it.

Visit your bank and ask what utility bills and others are direct-paid from the bank. Most of your utility bills, car payments, etc. can be deducted from your checking account. You'll have to authorize the creditors to take payments directly from your account each month. Federal laws prevent the creditor from taking more than you authorize.

You can also use the dreaded computer to track bills. Intuit's Quicken and Microsoft Money are fairly easy to use by downloading details of your financial transactions from banks and credit card accounts into your computer. They give you a way to plan and keep track of finances. You can tell immediately how much debt you have. They can remind you when bills are due and even worn you if your checking account is less than a desired level.

If' you're one of those out-of-control credit card people, consider consolidating the bills into one card. The more cards you use, the more interest rates, due dates and fees you have to track. Try to pay all possible on the card, and don't charge more than you can pay at the end of the month.

If you have several accounts such as IRA's, mutual funds, etc. at different banks, try to set them up into fewer accounts, preferably at one location. Keeping up with all of them is a problem if not consolidating. Some brokerages offer checking and savings accounts that are like ones at a conventional bank.

So, don't let money drive you crazy. It can be a great thing or devastate you. Think of money as a tool with which to find a treasure. A shovel is of no use to dig with if you never use it.

DEBT CONSOLIDATION CAN BE A FAST TRACK TO BANKRUPTCY COURT.

You've seen those stupid commercials on television that show people celebrating after they've consolidated their debts. They've consolidated things like credit card debts, car payments and house payments to arrive at a lower payment monthly. One lady says she had a swimming pool installed with the extra money she saved.

Consolidating several credit cards to only one card is different from using your home equity to put all your debts into one smaller payment. This is very dangerous and has not taught you how you got into the financial mess to begin with.

The sad truth is that people think debt consolidation is a free ticket out of debt. They owe less each month, but they now owe much longer than any of the consolidated bills would have taken to pay off. They may now owe fifteen years on that 1979 pickup truck they added to the total. It's also taken for granted that these people who got into this situation have suddenly learned not to do that anymore. Yeah, right!

This type of borrowing is foolish because it does nothing to solve the problem that caused it, overspending. You can't borrow yourself out of debt as long as you don't bring your spending habits under control. While you're paying that reduced monthly bill, you're still out there spending just like before. Now what are you going to do? Most of you probably used a home equity loan to swing the deal.

These types of loans are terribly expensive. They can be full of expensive insurance, hidden fees and other things that make it more profitable for the lender. If you haven't learned to control your spending habits, you're worse off, not better off.

Personal loans can offer as much as 15% interest rates for people with good credit. If you have bad credit, you could pay 21%. The more in debt you are, the higher interest rates you have to pay. This sounds backwards, doesn't it? The lender has to protect his company from your bad credit. You pay the price for not handling money correctly.

If you can obtain a low-rate loan and pay the debt off faster than you might otherwise, it may work for you. But most consumers look for lower payments, not lower costs. The total you will pay over a longer period of time will bankrupt you if you aren't careful.

If you get one of those consolidated loans and continue to run up big credit card balances afterward, you're coming closer to the financial brink of bankruptcy. Just as in buying an automobile, the lender may try to push you to borrow more, maybe for a vacation, etc. Don't fall for this. It's what got you into the mess in the first place. If your loan includes single premium credit insurance that covers the loan payments in case you get sick, die or become unemployed, a charge of up to $2000 may be added to the balance of a $5000 loan. That's sickening. You'll also pay interest on the insurance since it's tacked on up front. If you think the insurance amount of the payment seems small, maybe like $40 a month, multiply it times 48 or 60 months and add interest. The total will or should amaze you.

With consolidated loans, you may get the pitch that you can take a vacation from bills or a couple of months or more. Then you may be tempted to go back a year later and refinance again, with more insurance tacked on.

If your credit history is good, you may want to ask your credit card company to lower the rate. They may do this if you'll simply ask. You could even transfer balances to a lower rate card. Be careful, because applying for too many cards can hurt your credit.

Try paying yourself out of debt instead of debt consolidation. Pick the debt with the highest interest rate, and pay extra monthly on that one. When it's paid off, go to the next highest on. Work hard at this and enjoy the feeling of being debt free. Then, don't get back into the problem that plagued you before, overspending.

If you've convinced yourself that you must consolidate your debts, at least shop around. You'll find your options are quite different. Credit unions usually offer the best rates on personal loans. If you're so far in debt that you're considered a bad risk—in which case you need bankruptcy counseling or credit counseling instead of another loan—or you're in danger of becoming a victim of predatory lending.

Whether you consolidate or make the attempt to pay off your debts another way, you still must stop charging on credit cards if you expect to make progress. Just cut up the cards, freeze them in a block of ice or bury them outside. You must not have access to them if you're to refrain yourself to spend responsibly. If you need help, get help. Don't be bashful. Your financial future is at stake.

DOES INTEREST AND TIME REALLY MAKE THAT MUCH DIFFERENCE?

We've all argued with the car salesman about prices, but what about the interest % and the length of the loan? Some dealers now offer 84-month loans. That's seven years. Even at 0%, that's a lot of payments.

The same works with saving money. Time and interest are the key players. The result of saving a certain amount of money monthly for several years will surprise you. Look at the following chart to see the results of putting $100 a month into an account for specific periods of time.

Years	1%	2%	3%	4%
10	$12,725	$13,393	$14,108	$14,873
15	$19,527	$21,106	$22,854	$24,791
20	$26,678	$29,628	$33,012	$36,899
25	$34,195	$39,047	$44,812	$51,568
30	$49,454	$49,454	$58,519	$69,735
35	$50,405	$60,955	$74,441	$91,778
40	$59,138	$73,665	$92,937	$118,690

Years	6%	7%	8%	9%
10	$16,569	$17,509	$18,516	$19,596
15	$29,326	$31,980	$34,934	$38,224
20	$46,535	$52,496	$59,395	$67,389
25	$69,746	$81,580	$95,836	$113,053
30	$101,053	$122,809	$150,809	$184,547
35	$143,283	$181,256	$231,017	$296,484
40	$200,245	$264,112	$351,527	$471,743

Look carefully at those numbers. Notice the difference time makes, then look at the difference in money for just 1% difference in the interest rate. The quicker you begin to save, at whatever %, the larger the money will grow.

The contribution of $100 a month, once you commence to do it, will not be missed. You'll learn to do without it. Sit back and watch it grow, and grow and grow. If you are lucky enough to be young enough to take advantage of time, go for it. If not, start as soon as possible to get the maximum amount from the investment.

If you start with $100 a month and increase it by $50 a month each year, you could be looking at a very large retirement nest egg. Get your children interested by starting a small fund for them to show them the value of time and interest. They'll thank you for it.

WILL CASH REALLY BECOME OBSOLETE?

Many believe a cashless society is coming. It may, but it'll come a lot later than expected. They say we'll spend with a single plastic card that provides currency, identification and more. The fact that so many people have so little cash now has nothing to do with the cashless society. The cash is in the hands of others. Some have most of it.

Supposedly, a card embedded with microprocessor chips can be used for all cash type transactions. The American Express "blue card" has already been issued, but it appears that it is no better than a competitive credit card.

In 1994 the percentage of consumer purchases made with cash or checks was at 80%, compared with less than 66% now. Debit cards are widely used now. The chip card is loaded with a specific dollar value, and the amount of a purchase is deducted when a scan is made.

The technology exists for a cashless society, but there isn't much motivation for card users, merchants for consumers to use the chip cards as an alternative for cash. A good economic base for using the smart cards is difficult to make since the infrastructure is already built for credit cards and debit cards. They're also so inexpensive and reliable that a strong case away from them is hard to obtain. The other argument is the cost of producing the card with an embedded chip. It would cost more than six times the cost of a normal credit card. That equates to over $15 billion worldwide.

For the chip cards to be appealing to customers, it would have to make buying easier. And what is easier than using a credit card, or even writing a check? They'll have to hold personal information such as medical information so the hospital will know drug allergies, heart problems, etc.

Image a trip using only this new card. You gas up the car, pay the toll, pay for parking, get your boarding pass, eat at the airport, pay for food and hotels, etc. Then people will worry about security, everyone everywhere having access to all your information. This will be the big hurdle to overcome. If the card is lost or stolen, can you keep from losing the value stored on it? The worst fear may be if you forget your password.

Meanwhile, while we're waiting to move beyond cash, the government printing press is still humming, putting out around 9 billion new bills each year. A lot of it is to replace worn-out cash, and two thirds will satisfy demand for U.S. currency abroad.

I can just hear some people here in Georgia saying they are not giving up their cash. The day will come when you can't buy without one of these new cards. I was checking out of a Chicago hotel in 1980. A guy in front of me was trying to tell the clerk he had lost his credit card, and he would have to pay in cash. She said she couldn't take cash, only a credit card. The very upset man didn't know what to do. I asked him to give me the cash for his bill, and I'd put his bill and mine on my credit card. I now had several hundred dollars in my wallet. You can bet it wasn't begging to be spent. I secured it until I returned home and deposited it. After all, it was going to show up on my monthly bill.

Can you imagine going to a flea market or yard sale and springing one of the chip cards on them? You'd get looked at like the dog that stole the steak from the grill and laughed at for at least thirty minutes.

Hold onto your cash until you have to hold onto a funny looking little card. It's coming. Get ready for it. Until then, you can carry that fat wallet around and brag about all the money you have in it.

I CAN'T GO BROKE. I'M WORKING.

Do you think the only people in America who are broke have no jobs? So you think they went broke by not having money or possibly by spending beyond their means?

The mighty Casey Stengel once said you have to go broke three times to learn how to make a living. Think back at how many times you've been broke in your life. I don't mean the kind of broke when y you can't afford your next meal. I'm talking about reality here. If you're thirty years old and you have $500 to your name, you're broke. With $500 in the bank, you cloud lost your job and not be able to pay your next house and car payments.

Many people wonder how they went broke. They actually went broke gradually, then suddenly. It's possible to become broke instantly, but most people do it over a period of time without really noticing it. As long as they have enough money for today, they don't worry about tomorrow.

I've heard the expression, "I'm so broke I can't pay attention". Being broke means a wide range of ideas to us. Some may have thousands of dollars in the bank, and they still think they're broke. A rule of the thumb is to have at least six month's expenses in the bank. If that doesn't sound like much to you, think about it. If your family income is $33,000 annually, do you have $16,500 in your account? If you're unemployed for a long period of time, could you pay your bills and feed your family?

Someone put out a web site asking for financial help, that she was so broke she could not eat. She went on to say she and her husband both worked full time, and that she was pregnant. If she can't make a living now, what will she do when she is out of work to have the baby, and over half their income is gone? She needs to learn the lesson most people have to learn sometime in their lives, that you can't spend yourself out of debt. You must do everything in your power to keep from going broke. It's as if you're drowning and just quit trying to survive.

When driving through your town or city, look at the fine homes, the big cars and other things people just have to have. Then ask yourself if any of these people are broke. I'll tell you that most of them are either broke or very close to being broke. You must earn and bring home "more" than you owe. If this isn't the case with you, either earn more or spend less. The latter is easier.

The definition of broke is "penniless". Homeless people without a penny are broke. But you're also broke if you have mountains of bills to pay and can't pay them.

Having a roof over your head and a car in the driveway with seven gallons of gas in it doesn't mean you aren't broke. If you can't pay for groceries this week or your utility bills at month end, you're for all practical purposes broke.

The point I must make here is that it's easier to prevent becoming broke than to recover from it after it happens. Evaluate your situation by calculating how many weeks or months you have money to cover, if all your bills are more than your income and if you need to take a part-time job for a while to pay yourself out of debt. You must pay yourself out of debt, not spend your way out.

YOU DON'T JUST WAKE UP RICH ONE MORNING.

You can go broke much quicker than you can get rich, unless you win the lottery or inherit a fortune from your rich uncle. Rich doesn't mean wealth. What do you consider to be rich? How about wealthy?

If you investigated the topic of becoming wealthy, you'd find that wealth actually is accumulated over a lifetime of saving. The reason rich people get richer and poor people get poorer is that the rich keep doing what make them rich, and the poor keep doing the things that made them poor. You can do something about being broke, but it's not so easy to fix being poor.

You can repair being broke by working hard, saving some of what you earn, repeating the process over and over for a period of time. You finally won't be broke anymore, but you may still be poor. The poor will spend any amount they have, no matter how small or large, preventing them from accumulating wealth. Try giving a poor person a savings bond, cash or similar thing for their birthday, and see what they do with it. It'll all be spent before sundown. Others will put the bond away for it to grow and will save all or part of the cash.

If you were fairly deep in debt and inherited a large sum of money, would you pay off your debts and save the balance or go out on a spending spree and buy things that will Continue to leave you in debt.

Forget the lottery or a windfall from your family. Start now, today, this minute saving some of the money you bring home. You say you can't save, that you owe all you earn. If this is true, you're poor and broke. Saving a few dollars is better than none at all. After you see what a few dollars a week add up to in a few months, you'll be inspired to save more and buy less.

To properly save, you must start early and save often. Take advantage of time.

Don't contribute to your investments every six months or once a year. Invest regularly, at least once a month, if not once a week. You must be diligent. Don't loosen up and reduce your savings. You must invest through thick and thin, hard times and good times. Find a way to pay for unexpected expenses, but keep on track with your savings.

The truth is that you will or will not achieve wealth. You can find all the excuses in the world for not saving, but to achieve wealth you must get past your problems and excuses and just do it.

The next time you redeem a coupon for a dollar off, put that dollar into a jar, a drawer or your savings account. Take advantage of it. You'll save more than you imagine. Save all coins, just spend paper money. When you get paid, and before you pay your bills, pay yourself a few dollars. No matter what, don't give up this money to bills or other expenses. Save it, even though you may be broke afterward, but you've saved some money. Simply repeat the process and be amazed at how quickly it adds up.

Becoming wealthy over time is like building a house one room at a time. If you add one room each year, you'd retire with a 45-room house that you could sell for a fortune. Saving is fun and is much easier than you think. You just have to start sometime, and the time is night now.

HOW CAN I MAKE MORE MONEY? I'M ON TOP PAY NOW AT WORK.

I can't think of how many times I've heard people say they needed more money for bills, but that their paychecks just wouldn't go around. Bu wait. This is something you can do something about.

Take some quality time to figure our how to make more money (if you simply won't reduce your spending). Sit down in a quiet place with a pad and pen. Turn the television off. Get away from any distractions such as kids, pets or maybe even a spouse. Write down how much more money you want to earn in a week or a month. Be realistic. If your paycheck is $20, $40 or even $50 a week short of all your bills, try first to whittle down the bills. Then adjust your amount to be earned above your paycheck.

At first, you may not think of ways to earn more money. Start at a specific location, such as your home. You may think of ways to make things at home for sale. Many people make cookies, wedding cakes or other treats for sale at various places. Then think of outside the home, like your community. Do any of your neighbors need their grass cut or pruning or fertilizing done? If you can paint, do any neighbors need anything painted? If you're a handyman, you may get off jobs from your neighbors.

Before the 911 service came to my area, a guy in an old car came around with a few bags of concrete mix, a shovel, some black plastic piping and some lettering and numbering materials in his truck. For $20, he offered to dig a hole by your driveway, put a pipe into concrete, and put your name and address number on the pipe. This was so the 911 driver could find your residence. The guy was very motivated to earn money. Of course, the service was installed, and the same identifying pipes were offered from the 911 offices.

Your neighbors may need a babysitter or pet sitter or someone to go to the grocery store for them or haul off their garbage. With a pickup truck, you could haul many bags of garbage at once and set up trips on a weekly or bi-weekly basis. Only a few customers can net a pretty good amount of extra money.

If you're pretty good with a computer, you may want to set up a service in which you keep up with people's birthdays, anniversaries and other important dates. Then you would simply call or e-mail them before that important date arrives to remind them. Set up 100 such accounts for $5 a month each, and you've just added $500 a month to your earnings. This could be a payment on that new car. I've thought of this myself. Running an ad explaining the service may get you a lot of inquiries. Most people would love to let someone else keep up with that kind of stuff for them. If you already have a computer with Lotus or Excel on it and a phone, you're in business.

If you want to expand outside your neighborhood, start a pick-up service to buy groceries for people or maybe run errands to dry cleaners, pick up kids, etc. I know someone who has a van that holds about 10 kids. She simply picks up the kids at home, delivers them to school, and returns them home after school. With 10 kids at $3 a day, that's $150 a week, $600 a month. That would pay for the van and then some. Of course, do the legwork to see if you can get enough such clients to justify the cost.

If you have a chain saw and you're pretty good with it, drive around the neighborhood or the town to see how many limbs may be down after a storm. Most people will pay you to cut the limbs for them. You could also end up with a lot of firewood for the winter. This is hard, dirty work, but you can work at your own pace.

I had a bright idea once to buy an old tanker truck, like septic tank cleaners use, and mix up water with fertilizer in it. Then, I'd simply pull to the edge of the street and spray yards for people. I've noticed that the prettiest and best grass in some yards is where the washing machine has been run out through a pipe to a location in the yard. Believe me, this really happens. The ingredients in the powder or liquid cleaner seem to make grass greener, thicker and prettier. I thought I'd just mix washing powder or liquid cleaner with water and do the same with other yards. My wife said I'd probably kill somebody's expensive grass, though.

If you type or are good with a computer, you can get business writing essays and other reports for people. There is a lot of work out there and a lot of people who don't want to do it or can't do it.

My latest way to make money is to buy cars for people. Do you have any idea of the number of people who are horrified at the thought of facing that salesperson? Many people simply just pay the sticker priced and gets out of Dodge as soon as possible, after they've been through the bag of tricks and strategically impressive actions of the sales-person. If you let yourself be intimidated, you can buy a car you didn't want at a price you can't afford. With a computer, you can find the sites that show you the invoice, sticker and other information about any car or truck. Armed with this information, you can effectively make the best deal for an automobile. Run an ad stating that you'll go to the dealership to get the best deal possible for them. After the deal is made, simply take your clients to the dealership to finish the transaction. You then get a check from the client for 25% of the difference between the sticker price and the actual purchase price. You make 25% and the client saves 75% of the difference. With just a couple of trans-actions a week, you could pocket a sizeable amount of money.

Just look around and see the needs out there. Numerous people don't do things for reasons too many to mention. Some won't travel due to traffic or fear of driving. You may set up a time to transport them. An ideal trip service would be to and from the closest airport. People have a fear of driving there, parking and putting up with finding the right drop-off points. You could group as many as possible and make one or two trips a day.

Just think, think and think. You can come up with ways to earn more money if you really want to. It's up to you.

SOMETIMES YOU JUST HAVE TO THINK ON YOUR OWN.

Many people sit and wait for their expenses to decrease, like waiting for a crystal ball to tell you what to do. Folks, it isn't that easy. You must use that organ between your ears to achieve your cost reduction goals.

Start with your cable service for your television enjoyment. Look at all the stations you have. Do you really need 185 stations, including 45 sports stations, 32 music stations and about 26 movie stations? If so, why do you still rent movies? Do you really look at the extra channels enough to justify their expense? Does your wife know you have spent extra for Playboy? Start with the basic coverage, and if you really want more stations; add them on. Don't purchase an expensive package, only to settle to six or eight stations like I have.

Give up those membership clubs you belong to. Do you really benefit from them? Do you really need a trip planner or some of the other stuff they offer? A few dollars each month here and there will add up to substantial money.

Look into your homeowner's insurance policy. Some will require that the insured value of your interior furnishings be automatically equal to 1/3 of the insured value of the dwelling. If your home is insured for $100,000 and your furnishings have to be valued at 1/3 of the dwelling coverage, you will pay insurance on $33,000 worth of furnishings. Have you ever had that much stuff? Find an insurance company that will give you the option of choosing how much furnishings to cover, not to pay for some percentage determined by a computer as your dwelling value goes up. To save money, be sure to obtain replacement value on the home and furnishings. It'll cost you more initially, but if you have to replace them, you won't have to make up the large difference.

I can't get over the stupid phone rate advertising going on. If your rate per minute is really one of the most important bills you have, you have more problems than you admit. If saving a penny a minute will make or break you, you need to shut up the hole in your face and find something more satisfying to do with your time. Try to add up what you are really saving monthly. It'll probably be enough to buy a soda drink.

If your phone bills include all sorts of hidden and open fees, surcharges, etc., consider replacing your regular phone with a cell phone. Letting a cell phone serve for all your phone transactions is becoming quite popular. You can always have a phone handy, and if you're responsible with the way it's used, you can actually save money. When you move, you won't have to pay connection fees, etc. Don't go out and buy a package of 6000 minutes a month for a flat rate. I see far too many people around with a phone glued to their ear. Just use it responsibly.

LIVE WITHIN YOUR INCOME BY CUTTING COSTS.

If you've already decided that you won't seek additional earnings potential by doing work other than your normal job, you must now decide to cut costs to live within your income. That means your expenses must not exceed your income.

You must develop some sort of self-control of your spending. You've surely seen some families that seemed to manage their finances to get what they need and want. Those people probably will talk to each other about bills, income and how to live within their means. There will be a lot less worry about bills if the family communicates within to discuss upcoming expenses and how they will be paid.

Without knowing it, you actually plan to spend. If you're going to town to get a few items, you plan it. Planned spending must be done to achieve your goals on a fixed income. Your lifestyle will dictate your spending habits. If necessary, modify your life-style. You must know what your expenses are in order to control them. Write them down. Study them. Talk about them with other family members. Some people are afraid to look at them. They have some kind of idea if they ignore them, they'll go away.

If impulses take over when shopping for a major purchase, take a few breaths, walk away or go home if necessary. If impulse shopping costs you an extra $100 on an appliance purchase, you just spent your next month's utility bills.

Avoid shopping when you're depressed or down. It's easier to spend when you feel this way. Ask yourself why you're buying that particular product. If possible, wait for several sales when the prices are drastically reduced. Train yourself to go on a shopping trip with the intention of not buying anything that day, only to shop and compare prices. Take notes. Return later after you've decided what and which one you will purchase. Sure you've wasted some gas for the car, but you will save more than enough to compensate.

117

When buying clothing, coordinate the items. Look at care labels for fiber content and cleaning instructions. Take proper care of your clothing, and they will last longer, saving you money. If you owe installment debts with interest rates as high as 12-20%, consider taking money from your savings account to pay these bills. Your savings account may be paying .75% interest if you're lucky. Paying off a debt that has an interest rate much higher than the percent you're earning on your money is smart and will get you out of debt quicker. You can then return to your savings account and refrain from getting into those high interest bills again.

Try to insure your vehicles and your home at the same agency. You'll probably get a reduced rate for this. Always buy a homeowner's policy instead of different policies for fire, theft, etc. When paying premiums, pay them on an annual or six-month basis. You'll save money. It costs the insurance company to bill you monthly or quarterly.

Always keep a clean filter in air conditioning or furnace equipment. You'll save electricity and the life of the motors operating them. Conserve heat and cool air by using weather stripping, caulking and insulation.

Repair leaks within the home as soon as possible. They're annoying, expensive and will waste substantial amounts of water in a short period of time. It's amazing how much water can stream through a very small hole.

When watering your lawn, don't water the pavement and other non-grass areas. Too much is wasted and sent down the gutter each year. Don't set the sprinklers at warp sprinkling power. A slow watering is better.

Unless you specifically want all the frills of a very expensive appliance, the bottom-of-the-line model will work reasonably well. It's not just the extras on automobiles that cost us too much money, but also on other things we just have to have today.

Compare warranty coverage on appliances. The best way to save money is to avoid them. I told a salesman that if I needed extended maintenance coverage on that new refrigerator after only five years, his product wasn't worth buying anyway. These appliances should, and most do last 15-20 years or more.

CUTTING COSTS FOR WEDDINGS AND RECEPTIONS IS OKAY, TOO.

Some would shutter at the idea of cost cutting applied to that fabulous wedding to be and the reception to follow. If you can have just as beautiful a wedding and just as grand a reception by trimming a few corners, go for it.

If you're lucky enough to have daughters, you'll eventually face the dreaded wedding plans. I've been through it and know from experience that your pockets will be tremendously lighter after the wedding bills are paid.

If the wedding is around Valentine's Day, you can save a ton on chocolate hearts in bulk. You can even make your own and wrap them with supplies from a candy store. You can even buy the material for making your own pre-cut tulle or organza circles. A craft store can sell you a cutter.

For decorations, you can visit your local dollar store. That's right, I said it. Don't be shy. You don't have to tell all your secrets, do you? These stores have great process on ribbons, candles and other supplies. Ivy bowls and vases can also be found in discount stores.

Don't be afraid to use silk flowers instead of real ones. They look just as good and will last after real ones are gone. Also look in supermarkets for flowers. They'll be much cheaper than at a florist. You can be very frugal and grow your own flowers. Bridesmaids can carry flowers tied with a ribbon instead of carrying a bouquet. Use your imagination.

Make your own invitations. Craft or office supply stores carry kits. A CD may be available to show you how and help make them for you. You could save 50% or more by doing this.

If your family has a seamstress, as most families do, make your own dresses for the girls and ladies in the wedding. The boys and men may still be stuck with a tux or suit that fit when you tried it on a weed prior to the wedding, but it doesn't fit well at the wedding. After my daughter, Ginger's, wedding, I wrote a short story asking if the pants still fit after the wedding. This was from personal experience.

A wedding is to be beautiful, tearful and full of happy people. Why no make it at least a little happier for dad by cutting expenses and achieving the same results. I can tell you from personal experience that one month after the wedding, only four people will remember everything about it. After my daughter, Ginger's, wedding, I wrote a story about the pants not fitting after the wedding.

The reception is also to be grand and full of memories. Homemade items can save a lot of money and serve just as well. When my daughter married, I had made a macramé hanger for her. It was seven feet high with a brushed bottom. On one of the shelves, the bride and groom stood for everyone to enjoy. It just happens that they were actually Ken and Barbie dolls dressed in wedding clothing. Everyone complimented us on them and had no idea.

If weddings can save $2000 on a $6000 wedding, keep half the difference and give the newlyweds the rest for a great honeymoon. Then pray that you won't have more girl children late in life. Trust me, they're worth it. That special occasion will be just as special without the terribly expensive cost when you've added some frugality to it. They're just as married, and you aren't quite broke.

WE'RE HOW MUCH IN DEBT?

Have you ever added up your debts? Most people are afraid to do this. Your net worth is the difference in what you owe and what you have paid for or that is worth more than what is owed on it. When you put all the people in the country together, what do you think the total debt is?

It seems that we've been lulled into a false sense of security. It's time to get back to basics. The Federal Reserve Board stated that the national balance on credit cards, auto and other non-mortgage loans rose to a new record figure in April 2001 at $1.58 trillion dollars. That's $1,580 followed by nine zero's. Mortgage debt adds another $5.2 trillion dollars. That's a total of $6.78 trillion dollars.

Credit card delinquent payments rose to 5% delinquency. Mortgage delinquencies are also on the increase. Talk about biting off more than you can chew.

The worst indicator is an almost 20% increase in bankruptcies. It seems that each year shows a record for personal bankruptcies. The handwriting is on the wall. The good times have ended. It is time to get back to basics.

A $2000 big-screen television financed at 19.8% interest on a credit card with the minimum payment will require 31 years to pay off at more than $10,000. Interest alone is $8,000. This would require earnings of $12,000 to net $8,000 to pay the interest alone. You've just purchased the world's most expensive television.

If you were to put that same $8,000 of monthly payments of interest into a 10% mutual fund over the same 30 years, it would yield over $45,000 in personal wealth. You just gave it all up for that television.

Another way to look at this kind of spending is to say you pay monthly car payments for half of your working life. Let's say you pay $300 monthly. If that money were invested at 10%, you would have $227,800. That's $1,900 a month for the rest of your life. You've given up almost $2,000 monthly for the rest of your life by paying car payments by the month. The finance company is the only winner.

Other than mortgage and car payments, you need one simple rule to live by. And the rule is: If I can't afford something in cash, I can't afford to buy it. Practice it. Say it over and over every day. You will soon believe it and abide by it. Only then can you produce wealth.

Do you really want to know how much in debt you are? Before calculating it, write down the amount you think it is. Then write down car, house, credit cards, etc. and total it. You'll be amazed at the total. Then divide the number by your weekly take-home pay. This will tell you how many weeks you must work to pay off existing debts. As you add other debts to the total, the future looks very bleak, doesn't it?

So, keep saying to yourself, "If you can't afford to pay for it in cash, you can't afford it". Say it to your family members. Teach it to your kids. Tell it to your friends. You could even form a debt-a-holic group to discuss problems with bills and how to rid your-self of them. You must be honest with yourself and your family about how much debt you're in and how to get out of it. Just do it.

KIDS NEED TO LEARN MONEY MANAGEMENT, TOO.

We all know that kids really know how to spend money. They don't comprehend the work and sacrifice you endured to earn it. They expect it and don't care how it was earned, only that it's there when they want it.

I got an allowance when I was a boy. My brother and I had to do the chores, to be done with or without an allowance. Even small jobs or chores can teach a child the value of working for that money they expect. They'll learn how good working habits can influence their earning power. They will have an easier time finding jobs later and holding these jobs if they learn these lessons at home early in their lives. Show them how to save by opening up a savings account for them. Any small amount will teach them a valuable lesson. As the balance grows, they'll be more reluctant to spend.

Suggest to them that they should pay ¼ of their weekly allowance into the savings account. If they're into computers, and most are at six years of age, get them to keep a log of their expenses and their deposits. Set aside a time each week to discuss the savings program with them, and show them where they spent too much.

Your kids need to learn that you're not a walking cash machine. Don't simply hand money to them at each sudden impulse. Teach them that you can't always have what they want when they want it. Learn to say, "No".

When your kids go shopping with their allowance, set spending limits for them. Teach them that the most expensive things aren't always the best and that they don't have to impress anybody by spending too much.

Try this little trick to entice them to save. Put a quarter on the table. Beside it, place two dimes and a nickel, then five nickels in another, then twenty-five pennies in another. Tell them they can have any one stack of coins. You'll probably be surprised to see them take the five nickels. In their minds, they think this is more money, when it's actually more coins than the first two stacks. They may not take the pennies because of the bulk. They know the stacks are the same amount, but they see more in five coins than in one or two.

When my dad was well into his 40's, he had a safe deposit box. He would always put dollar bills in there. He had an amazing amount of dollar bills stacked up. I guess he thought that stack of bills looked like a lot of money. And it did. Sometimes, it's easier to save it if it looks like more.

Get children to do calculations involving money. Ask them to tell you how much money they would have saved if they had put $.25 a day into a jar for six months or a year. The answer will surprise them and teach them a valuable lesson about saving.

My son, when small, would ask me why a $10 bill was worth more than a $1 bill, that they were the same size. When I told him it took ten $1 bills to make one $10 bill, he began to understand. Then I'd have him with me at the drive-around window at the bank, and he'd thought I was giving the lady a note to give me some money, never thinking of where the money came from.

Do something great for your kids. Teach them about saving and spending. If you don't yet know this, learn and then teach them. You'll both be glad you did.

SAVE YOUR MARRIAGE BY SAVING YOUR FINANCES.

Not even the girl or guy next door can kill a marriage quicker than squabbles over money. If young people who haven't learned the value of money and how to hang onto it get married, it's a recipe for disaster.

Young married people seem to want everything at once, not knowing it takes a long time to obtain the things we want or need. First, they probably don't know how to make a budget. They have no idea of how much the bills will amount to. As young workers, they probably won't earn much money for a few years, but they want everything now.

Holidays seem to be the culprit most of the time. They haven't learned that you don't buy if you don't have the money to do so. I've heard of some who took loans from their 401k programs to buy Christmas toys for the kids. This is the worst of all mistakes and will ruin you financially. Thank God most of them don't qualify for a credit card.

The reason young married people won't admit they have money problems may be that they are afraid of rejection. They keep secrets and won't admit the reality of their situation. They may hide credit card bills. Sometimes, it's just the fear of the unknown. They just don't want to face reality.

I've seen young people who didn't have a checking or savings account. They spent from the pocket. No wonder the bills never get paid. When those who do have a checking account get into trouble, it's usually because nobody is balancing the check-book. They're not recording all their checks and the balance. They should get a ledger book and post the date, check number, check amount, reason for the check and the ending balance. This will let them know how much they have and slow down the spending. As a parent, buy the ledger book, take it to them, show them how to set it up, and regularly ask them if they are maintaining it.

Some spouses give the paycheck over to the other and never look at what happens to it. The person handling the bill paying may or may not be paying them. When trouble comes, there's usually a cover-up by the person paying the bills. It can go as far as to ruin their credit or even cause a marriage break-up.

Ask any young married person what they argue about the most, and they'll tell you it's money. When married, both must talk over purchases, go over bank accounts, and be open with each other about spending. If there's $120 in the bank, the husband shouldn't go out and buy a new deer stand, leaving the utility bills unpaid. Neither should the wife buy new shoes and jeopardize the bills waiting to be paid.

One point I tried to drive home with my kids was that bills come first. That's not your money. Even if you're left flat broke, the bills must be paid, no matter what. Sit at home and watch television and eat microwave dinners if necessary until all comes back into balance. Some watch their bank balances grow throughout the month, thinking they're okay, then make the car and house payments, only to find themselves broke again. Bills due on a monthly basis must be paid weekly to the checking account. Once you deposit it, it's not yours to spend. You can't dip into that fund. It's already owed to creditors.

Most money problems occur because people don't talk about money before they get married. Before marriage, sit down together and go over total income and upcoming expenses. Talk about any credit card problems and debts. Talk about bank accounts, savings and checking. Then talk about how you will set up a savings account, how you feel about contributions to a 401k program at work and who should manage the money in the relationship. Hopefully, both of you will.

Statistics show that over 50% of marriages end in divorce and that most of the time it's because of fighting over money. That's the reason you get all this out front prior to marriage. Don't be shy. If there are any problems to work out, it's better to discuss them before than after marriage. When the creditors are calling and knocking on your door, the fight over money can't be far behind.

I heard of a couple going in to see a marriage counselor. They were spending almost $1000 a month on over-the-limit charges and late fees on credit cards. They had 17 credit cards, a beautiful home and very nice cars. The problem was so bad they weren't even speaking to each other. There was probably enough blame to go around. Both of them let this problem get completely out of hand. This couple wasn't speaking, being intimate with each other and was on the edge of a divorce.

Such problems will lead to actually falling out of love with each other. This disaster should have never come to this point. How could it have been stopped earlier? Talking to each other may have prevented it. Both partners should talk about money issues often to stay on top of their problems and solve them.

A good start for such couples is to begin with getting rid of the credit cards. They still have the debt to pay off. They just won't be charging bigger balances. If only one card is kept for an emergency, the card should not be kept on the person. It should be put away from your wallet or purse to avoid the impulse to use it.

By dialing the credit card companies and telling them you have good intentions, but that you may not be able to pay the debt with such high interest, they usually lower the rate so you can continue to give them money. Just try it. It works for many, many people. If you can get them to reduce the rate form 22% to 10%, you'd be amazed at eht quicker time to pay the debt.

To reduce debt and save the marriage, talk, talk and talk. Sit down and write on a pad the things you can do without. If you're making calls every hour on a cell phone, stop it. Cell phones are for emergencies, not gossiping or just chatting. If you have a computer and on the Internet, use e-mail to make those long distance calls. Look at how you buy groceries. Don't buy pre-packaged food. Cut your own children's hair. You don't own stock in the barbershop or beauty shop. Stop eating out for a while, then limit it. Don't have pizza delivered every day. If you drink a lot of coffee at work, make it at home and take it to work.

Desperate times demand desperate measures. Get with the program. Save your marriage by being responsible and sharing financial problems with each other. Make a promise to each other that money will not cause you to break up. Do whatever is needed to cut expenses. Then reserve one night every two weeks to get out, away from kids and the house, to enjoy each other and get repairs made to the marriage.

There are a lot of counselors out there because there are a lot of marital problems out there, and most of them involve money. Don't be a victim. Get started now and early to confront money problems, learn to fix them, and share your lives in the way it was intended to be.

GET OUT OF TOWN.

We've discussed saving, avoiding unnecessary expenses, etc. Now let's discuss something we all want, most do, and many wished they could do. Let's talk about taking a vacation. If you are going to take a vacation, heck or high water, you must be prepared for it and for the possible money problems resulting from it if your spending gets out of hand.

When you decide where, when and how long your vacation will be, the work has just begun. The next step is to try to find the money to take the trip. If you don't have it put aside, start now to create a vacation savings plan. To do this you must itemize the costs associated with the trip. Determine the time from now until the date of departure, divide the time into numbers of weeks, and see if you can possibly save that much each week. If not, you have choices. You can cancel the trip, go later or take the cheaper trip.

If you've got the Internet, do your homework. Look at all the information you can handle to get the best prices. You'll be amazed at the difference in the same vacation on different sites. An all-inclusive trip such as flight, room, food, etc. could save a bundle. It may be cheaper to fly somewhere for a few days than to drive for days and spend less time at your destination. At least, you eat on the plane and probably will get a continental breakfast with the package each day.

A cruise could be a very pleasurable trip. You don't have to drive for days. The food is included. You'll see more sights, have more recreation and get more quality time with the spouse and maybe the kids than any other way. This could be cheaper than driving to the beach for a week. The probability of the marriage staying intact may increase, too.

Don't forget about food and souvenirs. You don't want to return with a massive credit card headache. If you are driving on the vacation, take a cooler and some food along. It'll be more convenient and much cheaper. When you're settled in your room, use your cooler to store drinks bought at a local store, not from the vending machines. If your cooler isn't too big, the hotel ice machine will come in handy.

If you must cut expenses to save for a vacation, do it. It'll teach you something that will stay with you after the vacation is history. You may save enough the next year so that you don't have to set up a special account for the vacation.

My wife and I spent a week on Maui years ago. She asked if I was going to come to bed. My answer was that I couldn't afford to sleep in a place that costly, that I wanted to stay awake all possible and get my money's worth.

If your vacation destination offers a free continental breakfast, take advantage of it. Muffins and fruit aren't bad for you, and the rest of the day may be more pleasurable, too. If you're in a resort, don't eat there. Go elsewhere to get better prices and see the sights.

A very easy way to afford that annual trek is to have about $12 weekly or $50 monthly withdrawn from your paycheck and direct deposited to a Christmas club account at a local bank or credit union. You'll have a little over $600 at the end of the twelve months, just in time to take the vacation. You won't miss the money and won't have to come up with all the money at once.

If taking that annual trip we call vacation digs into your bill money, take a few breaths, sit down, plan a couple of days of eating our, plan a backyard cookout and enjoy yourself. If you think the vacation was all that important, get your finances in line to allow you to take one. It's your fault you got into that situation, anyway.

I heard news that fourteen days of complete relaxation, with no work or worries, may reduce your IQ by as much as twenty points. A few weeks like this, and you won't be able to work and won't have to worry about the expense of a vacation.

SET UP THAT EMERGENCY FUND.

I've heard it called "rat hole money, "emergency money", etc. If you think that $20 stuffed back into your wallet or purse is an emergency fund, you're in trouble. In fact, if you don't have an emergency fund amounting to at least three months worth of living expenses, you're in trouble.

I know, I know. You are asking how you can have three months of bills in an emergency fund when you can barely pay your bills. You're not alone. Very few people have this much money. That's the reason Americans are basically broke and will retire broke.

If you become unemployed or hurt and out of work, think of how much you would have to have to just break even. You'd have to pay insurance premiums that normally come out of your paycheck. You'd have to have food, house and car payment money. You even have to continue to pay your life insurance.

Emergency money must be accessible. That brings on the problem of possibly dipping into it. If you're not disciplined, you can easily tap into it for impulse buying. If you dip into it, you must repay it as soon as possible. You may want to use a short-term CD account to hold it. The interest won't be much, but it'll be harder to get to than if it is in the top drawer of your chest of drawers.

If you keep it in an additional bank account, don't let it fall below the minimum required to avoid fees, etc. If you're fortunate enough to not need the emergency fund or a year or so, don't just go and spend it. Continue to maintain it to a larger cushion. This will teach you to save and be more aware of your needs.

When you hear people say they aren't broke, that they have $800 in the bank, ask them how long that money would last if they were unemployed or sick or hurt and out of work for a long period of time. Their answer will surprise them and open their eyes to the fact that the longer you work, the more you should save, and that the amount you have saved becomes a smaller percentage of the total money you've made over the years.

If you invest in coins or some other things that grow in value, it isn't money ill spent. If the time ever comes when you need to come up with money for expenses, the collection could get you over the hump. After all, it probably increases in value more than interest on a savings account.

When you do start an emergency fund, decide what an emergency really is. It's not that trip to the video store or that spur of the minute trip to the mountains for a weekend. It's truly for an emergency.

If your living expenses are $2000 monthly, you will need at least $6000 in your emergency fund. You gasp for air and wonder how in the world you could save that much. Well, sit and write down the things you spend money on that you shouldn't have or didn't have to, and you'll see it easier than you thought.

If you're the type that doesn't worry about what may happen or just don't want to think about it, then this lesson isn't for you. But at least I got you to think about it. And I'll bet the more you think about it, the more you may think of how necessary it is. Go ahead and try it. You may surprise yourself.

QUOTES FOR FRUGAL LIVING

Sometimes a quote or a few words can be as important and impressive as a whole volume of books. People who know what frugal living means have quotes about it and what is really wise and important in life.

Franklin D. Roosevelt said, "Happiness lies in the joy of achievement and the thrill of creative effort".
Albert Einstein said, "The more I learn, the more I realize I don't know".
An unknown said, "If grass is greener on the other side of the fence you can bet the water bill is higher".
Frank Gelett Burgess said, "If in the last few years you haven't discarded a major opinion or acquired a new one, check your pulse, you may be dead".
An ancient proverb says, "Good habits result from resisting temptation".
Wayne Gretzky said, "I miss 100% of the shots I never take".
Aristotle said, "We are what we repeatedly do. Excellence, then, is not an act, but a habit".
Mike Todd said, "I've never been poor—only broke. Being poor is a frame of mind. Being poor is only a temporary situation".
William J. Bryant said, "Destiny is not a matter of chance, it is a matter of choice. It is not a thing to be waited for, it is a thing to be achieved".
Les Brown said, "Shoot for the moon. Even if you miss, you'll land among the stars".
Henry Ward Beecher said, "It is the heart that makes a man rich. He is rich according to what he is, not according to what he has".
A marketing director said, "We've been doubling sales every 18 months. However, when you start form zero, it takes a long while".
Sidney Madwed said, "The finest gift you can give anyone is encouragement. Yet, almost no one gets the encouragement they need to grow to their full potential. If everyone received the encouragement they need to grow, the genius in most everyone would blossom and the world would produce

abundance beyond our wildest dreams".

Dale Carnegie said, "Most of the important things in the world have been accomplished by people who have kept on trying when there seemed to be no hope at all".

Yogi Berra said, "You can observe a lot by just watching".

Yogi also said, "If you come to a fork in the road, take it".

Someone said, "When you feel yourself coming to the end of your rope, tie a knot in it".

Someone said "There's a fine line between fishing and standing on the shore and looking like an idiot".

Antoine St. Exupery said, "If you want to build a ship, don't drum up the men to gather wood, divide the work, and give orders. Instead, teach them to yearn for the vast and endless sea".

Someone said, "Have nothing in your house that you don't know to be useful to be beautiful".

Derek Bok said, "If you think education is expensive, try ignorance".

After a waitress asked Yogi Berra if he wanted his pizza cut into four or eight pieces, he said, "Four, I don't think I can eat eight".

Poga said, "We are confronted with insurmountable opportunities".

Ray Comfort said, "Never let the defeat of the past rob you of the success of your future".

An Arabian proverb says, "You won't gain knowledge by drinking ink".

Thomas Jefferson said, "I find that the harder I work, the more luck I seem to have".

Thomas Alva Edison said, "If we all did the things we are capable of doing we would literally astound ourselves".

Winston Churchill said, "Man will occasionally stumble upon the truth, but most of the time he will pick himself up and continue on".

Henry Ford said, "Failure is merely another opportunity to more intelligently begin again".

Someone said, "Too many people live by the clock and leave their hearts slumbering in bed when it's time to go to work".

Dale Carnegie said, "You never achieve real success unless you like what you are doing".

An author said, "There's no substitute for getting smarter, faster. Try stuff. See what works. See what fails miserably. Learn. Rinse. Repeat.

When New York mayor Lindsay's wife said to Yogi Berra on a hot day, "You look nice and cool, Yogi", Yogi said, "You don't look so hot yourself".

Confusius said, "He who does not economize will have to agonize".

Robert Lewis Stevenson said, "Everyone who got where he is had to begin where he was".

Francis H. Bradley said, "The secret of happiness is to admire without desiring".

Voltaire said, "Common sense is not so common".

John Verdant said, "You vote for the kind of economy, society and environment that you want every time you spend green ballots called money".

Napolean Hill said, "The starting point of all achievement is desire".

J.M. Barrie said, "It is not real work unless you would rather be doing something else".

Yogi Berra said, "A nickel isn't worth a dime anymore".

Katherine Graham said, "To love what you do and feel that it matters—how could any-thing be more fun"?

Coleman Cox said, "I am a great believer in luck. The harder I work the more of it I seem to have".

Alexander Graham Bell said, "When one door closes, another opens; but we often look so long and so regretfully upon the closed door that we do not see the one which has opened for us".

Theodore Rubin said, "The problem is not that there are problems. The problem is expecting otherwise and thinking that having problems is a problem".

Dale Berra (Yogi's son) said, "The similarities between me and my father are different".

Nathaniel Bronner said, "Madison Avenue will promise us anything, make us want anything, then deliver us anything—the Mad in Madison Avenue may indicate that you've got to be crazy to believe everything that advertising tells you".

Someone said, "Life is a do-it-yourself project".

Don D. Pagan said, "I'm probably as dumb as I was 20 years ago except I just know how to cover it up a little better".

Rush Limbaugh said, "The solution to the nation's problems depends on the true American achievers. It's people like you, playing by the rules and celebrating and continuing to remind people of the traditions and institutions that made this country great, who can re-create a society that is great once more. It's only by doing the right thing that this country is going to fix itself and survive".

C. Elijay Bronner said, "Be thankful for the vision, no matter how imperfect it may be, but don't hide under the table when you realize that you're wearing mismatched socks".

Someone said, "The only difference between a rut and a grave is the depth".

Franklin D. Roosevelt said, "There are many ways of going forward, but only one way of standing still".

George W. Bush said, "These acts shattered steel, but they cannot deny the steel of American resolve".

Mahatma Gandhi said, "The future depends on what you do in the present".

Bill Cosby said, "You can turn painful situations around through laughter. If you find humor in anything—even poverty—you can survive it".

Douglas Noel Adams said, "When you blame others, you give up the power to change".

Rosalyn Carter said, "You have to have confidence in your ability, and then be tough enough to follow through".

Millard Fuller said, "It's not your blue blood, your pedigree or your college degree. It's what you do with your life that counts".

Kobi Yanada said, "Sometimes you just have to take a leap, and build your wings on the way down".

Someone said, "Things which matte most should never be at the mercy of things which matter least".

Tom Cooper said, "No one is worthless; we can all use a bad example".

Johnathan Kozol said, "Pick battles important enough to fight and small enough to win".

A LITTLE SAVVY SPENDING QUIZ

Here's a little quiz to determine if you have or do not have spending savvy. Take time to take it and see how you look compared to how you thought you looked.

When you receive your paycheck, you:
Have 401k money skimmed off the top and save for college expenses, etc.
Pay off bills accumulated since your last paycheck.
Go on a shopping spree, paying bills later.
Put your whole check into savings.

When you plan your yearly vacation, you:
Wait until the last minute and feel you've spent too much, deciding it isn't worth it.
Decide you can't spare the money.
Use money you've set aside in the budget for leisure.
Say your job is stressful and that you need a vacation to relax, no matter the cost.

Which of the following offers the highest interest rate?
Treasury bills
Money market mutual fund
Bank certificates of deposit
Bank money market account

When your favorite store announces a going-out-of-business sale, you:
Look at your credit limits on your cards and plan to spend big.
Think of what you planned to buy and decide which you buy.
Stay at home. You don't trust yourself to control spending.
Buy what you want and skip the vacation next year.

Which describes the way you purchase things?

You've noticed a spending pattern when you're happy or sad.

You worry that you don't have things your friends have, so you play catch-up.

You are a cycle spender, running up credit card bills, and paying them down.

You budget for spending, allowing for a few extras, generally sticking to your list.

When it comes to credit card interest rates, you take what you can get.
18%
6% because you switch cards to lower introductory rates every few months
10%, but it doesn't matter because you pay the monthly balance when due

How much of your income do you save?
Nothing
10-15%
50%
2-3%

When you get a raise, you typically:
Go on a shopping spree.
Don't notice.
Promise yourself again that you will prepare a budget.
Treat yourself to dinner out and buy something you've been waiting for and then save the balance.

Add up your debt except food and utilities. What % of your monthly income is it?
50%
40%
35%
20-25%

When you think about your financial situation, you feel:
Confident—you're meeting your goals you set.
You think about it only late at night when you can't sleep.
Hopeless—it seems you keep falling further and further behind.
Optimistic—you're buying lots of things and will begin to start saving soon.

Your friend calls about a once-in-a-lifetime fishing trip. You have no extra $.

You

Review your credit card balances and try to get enough from cash advances.

Decline and promise yourself that you'll start a fishing fund.

Accept. You'll figure out details later.

Decide to take a loan from your 401k, your dad, your girlfriend. You've got to go.

It's Christmas time again. You:

Vow you won't overspend by as much as last year.

Apply for more credit cards.

Get drunk. You're still paying from last year and your cards are charged to the limit.

Pull out the budget from last year, inflate it by consumer price index or your raise.

As your monthly bills come in, you:

Don't notice. You have arranged for automatic bill paying at the bank.

Pay the minimum on each one and throw it in the trash.

Put them off until the second notice and then pay the minimum.

Pay them once a month.

You get the dreaded pink slip at work. You:

Try to arrange for higher credit limits and a home equity loan.

Plan that vacation you haven't had time for.

Go on a shopping spree to cheer yourself up.

Arrange for continued medical benefits from the company and, while worried, at least pat your self on the back for having an emergency fund.

You have just been offered your first fob after graduation from college. You:

Arrange for lines of credit.

Borrow from your parents to buy a new wardrobe and a new car.

Decline to sign up for the company's 401k plan—retirement is a long way away.

Draw up a budget and arrange to save 10% of your salary.

You're expecting your first child. You:

Buy a bigger home.

Draw up a new budget.

Treat your self to the last summer vacation you'll have as childless.

Feel depressed; you're not successful enough financially to be a parent.

Over 10 years, which investment portfolio is likely to earn the best return?
100% bank certificates of deposit
50% stocks, 50% bonds
40% stocks, 30% bonds, 30% treasury bills
85% stocks, 15% bonds

You've received an inheritance of $100,000. You:
Go on a trip around the world.
Quit your job and start a business you're wanted to start for years.
Adjust your portfolio of stocks and bonds, making it a little more conservative.
You don't need to take so many risks now that you have more money.
Feel anxious. Dad didn't enjoy his life because he was always scrimping.
He was always saving to leave that money for you.

You're looking for a new home. You:
Go for broke; you'll grow into the payments.
You've been shopping for years, but you can't make such a commitment.
Realize you'll never own a home. Your credit rating is severely impaired.
Decide how much house you can afford before you shop and stick with it.

When making a large purchase, you typically feel:
Satisfied—you did your researching and planning for it.
Elated—then down.
Depressed—you don't deserve anything that costs that much.
Regretful—you didn't make the right decision.

JOKES ABOUT MONEY TO CHEER YOU UP

Depression

A businessman was in a great deal of trouble. His business was failing, he had put every-thing he had into the business, he owed everybody—it was so bad he was contemplating suicide. As a last resort he went to a priest and poured out his story of tears and woe.

When he had finished, the priest said, "Here's what I want you to do: Put a beach chair and a Bible in your car and drive down to the beach. Take the beach chair and the Bible to the waters edge, sit down in the chair and put the Bible in your lap. Open the Bible; the winds will rifle the pages, but finally the open Bible will come to rest on a page. Look down at the page and read the first thing you see. That will be your answer to tell you what to do".

A year later the businessman returned to the priest and brought his wife and children with him. The man was wearing a custom tailored suit, his wife in a mink coat, the children shining. The businessman pulled an envelope stuffed with money from his pocket, gave it to the priest as a donation in thanks for his advice.

The priest recognized the benefactor, and he was curious. "You did as is suggested"? he asked.

"Absolutely", replied the businessman.

"You went to the beach"?

"Absolutely".

"Yu sat in the beach chair with your Bible in your lap"?

"Absolutely".

"You let the pages rifle in the wind until they stopped turning"?

"Absolutely".

"And what were the first words you saw"?

"It read, Chapter 11".

Wise uncle Rusty

Uncle Rusty is a wise man. A while back he retired and purchased a modest home near a junior high school. He spent the first few weeks of this retirement in peace and quite, puttering around his workshop.

This is, of course, until the school year began. On the first day of school, three young boys, full of vented up energy from a full day of school, came down the street. As they walked down the street, they beat rhythmically on every garbage can on the street. Day after day, it was the same thing. Beating, clanging and pounding out a rhythm on the cans as they walked down the street; the noise continued. Poor uncle Rusty just couldn't take it anymore.

The next afternoon, he walked out to meet the young musicians. As they worked their way down the street, pounding out a tune on the cans, Rusty stopped them and said, "You kids sure are having a lot of fun. I like seeing young people like you express themselves. In fact, I used to do the same thing when I was your age. Will you do me a favor? I'll give you each a dollar if you come around every day and do your thing". The kids were elated and continued to do a bang-up job on the garbage cans.

After two days, uncle Rusty greeted the kids again, but this time he had a sad expression on his face. I'm having some financial trouble, and I'll only be able to pay you $.50 each to beat the cans".

The boys were not pleased, but they did accept his offer and continued their afternoon concert. A couple of days later, sly uncle Rusty approached them again as they drummed their way down the street.

With words that would ensure he would have peace and quiet from that day forward, he said, "Look, my social security check just isn't stretching as far with the expenses. So, I'm only going to be able to pay you $.25 each day. Will that be okay"?

The leader of the boys exclaimed, "If you think we're going to waste our time beating those cans around for a quarter, you're nuts! No way, mister, we quit".

The art collector

A famous art collector is walking through the city when he notices a mangy cat lapping mild from a saucer in the doorway of a store. He does a double take.

He knows that the saucer is extremely old and very valuable, so he walks casually into the store and offers to buy the cat for two dollars.

The owner of the store replies, "I'm sorry, but the cat isn't for sale".

The collector says, "Please, I need a hungry car around the house to catch mice. I'll pay you twenty dollars for that cat".

And the owner says, "Sold", and hands over the cat.

The collector continues, "Hey, for twenty bucks I wonder if you could throw in that old saucer. The cat's used to it and it'll save me from having to get a dish".

The owner says, "Sorry, but that's my lucky saucer. I've sold sixty-eight cats this week".

Donkey raffle

A Cajun named Jean Paul moved to Texas and bought a donkey from an old farmer for $100. The farmer agreed to deliver the donkey the next day. The next day, the farmer drove up and said, "Sorry, but I've got bad news. The donkey died last night".

"Well, just give me my money back".

"I can't do that. I went and spent it already".

"Okay then, just unload the donkey".

"What do you want with a dead donkey"?

"I'm going to raffle it off".

"You can't raffle off a dead donkey".

"Sure I can. Watch me. I just won't tell anybody that he's dead".

A month later, the farmer met up with the Cajun and asked, "What happened with the dead donkey"?

"I raffled him off. I sold 500 tickets at $2 each and made a profit of $998".

"Didn't anybody complain"?

"Just the guy who won. I gave him his $2 back".

Expensive doctors

A young woman wasn't feeling well, asked one of her co-workers to recommend a physician.

"I know a great one in the city, but he's very expensive. He charges $500 for the first visit and $100 for each one after that".

The woman went to the doctor's office and, trying to save a little money, cheerfully announced, "I'm back".

Not fooled for a second, the doctor quickly examined her and said, "Very good, just continue the treatment I prescribed on your last visit".

Insufficient funds

A young co-ed came running in tears to her father. "Dad, you gave my some terrible financial advice"!

"I did. What did I tell you"?

"you told me to put my money in that big bank, and now that big bank is in trouble".

"What are you talking about" That's pone of the largest banks in the state", he said.

"I don't think so. They just returned one of my checks with a note saying, insufficient funds".

MAKE THAT GARAGE SALE A BIG SUCCESS.

Let's assume you really want to have a great garage sale. To properly pull it off, you must do your homework. First, ask why you want to have the sale. Is it because you've accumulated too much "stuff" around the house? Is it because you want to turn "stuff" into a few dollars? Or is it because you need money quickly and want to make as much as possible?

Timing is everything. Don't do it during a holiday period. People are either going out of town or need their money for some sort of celebration at home. Most garage sales run from spring through fall. Check the weather forecasts days in advance. You don't want to cancel the sale or throw all of it into boxes when the rains come. Saturdays are the best time for such sales. People are usually out milling around, and they've just been paid.

You may want to incorporate the sale with neighbors. More "stuff" will draw a larger crowd, and you'll need the additional parking spaces anyway. The expenses of putting on the sale can then be split with the neighbor(s). Be careful to not get too big or the competition can be harmful to your sale. Ask the neighbors what type "stuff" they will sell.

Don't be pushy. If a person beams in on something, let them look. If they start to walk away, ask what they will give for the item. Look into the eyes of the potential buyers. You can usually tell if they're really interested. If someone offers a price that is ridiculously low for something, calmly say you can't possibly take that for it.

Have bags and boxes on hand. Most people will ask if you have a bag or something since they may find other things they like. Accommodate the buyers. Be friendly and get used to the fact that there will be a loud-mouthed fanatic in the crowd before the day ends.

Advertising can really make the sale a success. Show a sample of the things for sale. Make the ad long enough to draw attention to it. Give directions. A small percent of people in your town know where you live. Place signs from your home outward about a mile to lead people there. Be sure the ad is eye-catching and long enough. You may only have to sell a couple of items to pay for it.

A month or so before the sale, take a pad and pen into each room, the basement, the attic, in the out-building and under the house if necessary. Make a detailed listing of each item you will want to add to the sale. List the items per room so gathering them later will be easier. While making the list, write down what you want to sell them for. You can then check your list when someone asks what you want for an item. Think about what you would pay for the item is you went to such a sale.

Appliances that are in good working order should bring about ¼ their original cost. Try to have the instruction manuals with them. This impresses the buyer and lets them know you kept the appliance in good working order.

Make the day a pleasurable one. Have snacks and drinks on hand. Soft drinks bought for $.20 each on sale can sell for $50 each on a hot day. Cookies are also desirable. Learn from the experience. Write down things you learned and be prepared for the next great sale. You'll be amazed at how much money this type of sale can generate.

THAT'S IMPOSSIBLE.

I know you've often asked yourself, your spouse, your kids, your dog, your cat, your neighbors, your invisible friend and others where the other money went that you thought you had. This money seems to disappear somehow. Let's look at three scenarios. Assume you work 40 years and get a 3% increase yearly. The three starting annual pay amounts are $25,000 and $35,000. You should fit in there somewhere.

Year	annual pay	take-home	annual pay	take-home
1	$25,000	$17,000	$35,000	$23,800
2	$25,750	$17,510	$36,050	$24,514
3	$26,523	$18,035	$37,132	$25,249
4	$27,318	$18,576	$38,245	$26,007
5	$28,138	$19,134	$39,393	$26,787
6	$28,982	$19,708	$40,575	$27,591
7	$29,851	$20,299	$41,792	$28,418
8	$30,747	$20,908	$43,046	$29,271
9	$31,669	$21,535	$44,337	$30,149
10	$32,619	$22,181	$45,667	$31,054
11	$33,598	$22,847	$47,037	$31,985
12	$34,606	$23,532	$48,448	$32,945
13	$35,644	$24,238	$49,902	$33,933
14	$36,713	$24,965	$51,399	$34,951
15	$37,815	$25,714	$52,941	$36,000
16	$38,949	$26,485	$54,529	$37,080
17	$40,118	$27,280	$56,165	$38,192
18	$41,321	$28,098	$57,850	$39,338
19	$42,561	$28,941	$59,585	$40,518
20	$43,838	$29,810	$61,373	$41,733

21	$45,153	$30,704	$63,214	$42,985
22	$46,507	$31,625	$65,110	$44,275
23	$47,903	$32,574	$67,064	$45,603
24	$49,340	$33,551	$69,076	$46,971
25	$50,820	$34,557	$71,148	$48,380
26	$52,344	$35,594	$73,282	$49,832
27	$53,915	$36,662	$75,481	$51,327
28	$55,532	$37,762	$77,745	$52,867
29	$57,198	$38,895	$80,077	$54,453
30	$58,914	$40,062	$82,480	$56,086
31	$60,682	$41,263	$84,954	$57,769
32	$62,502	$42,501	$87,503	$59,502
33	$64,377	$43,776	$90,128	$61,287
34	$66,308	$45,090	$92,832	$63,126
35	$68,298	$46,442	$95,617	$65,019
36	$70,347	$47,836	$98,485	$66,970
37	$72,457	$49,271	$101,440	$68,979
38	$74,631	$50,749	$104,483	$71,048
39	$76,870	$52,271	$107,617	$73,180
40	$79,176	$53,839	$110,846	$75,375
totals	$1,185,031	$1,281,821	$2,639,044	$1,794,550

Now, let's look at probable bills you'll owe during the 40 years.

House	$180,000
Automobiles	$96,000
Groceries	$166,000
Electricity	$36,000
Water	$7,200
Phone	$14,400
Cable television	$24,000
Auto insurance	$20,000
House insurance	$16,000
Auto taxes	$3,000
House taxes	$16,000
Auto maintenance	$15,000
House maintenance	$12,000
Recreation	$20,000
Clothing	$40,000
Doctors	$12,000

Medicine	$5,000
Dentists	$12,000
Vacations	$16,000
School expense	$13,000
Birthdays	$15,000
Christmas	$14,000
Anniversary	$4,000
Miscellaneous	$42,000
Grand total	$799,000

Now, lets compare the take-home pay with expenses. If you take home $1,281,821 and owe $799,000, the difference is $482,821. That's $12,000 a year. Where did it go? If you take home $1,794,550 and owe $799,000, the difference is $$995,550. That's $25,000 a year. Where did it go?

Does this conclude that the more we earn, the more we spend? Do your expenses double from scenarios one and two?

Try to add bills and other expenses to the list and do your own math. You still can't explain where all that extra money went.

Can you imagine how much you could retire on if you had put the extra money into stocks, etc.?

This is why my wife doesn't work outside the home. You just can't imagine how many dollars are wasted on trivial stuff and things we just have to have.

Take another look at the earnings and take home pay numbers. Scenario two starts out earning $10,000 more than number one. After 40 years, the difference is over $30,000.

Investing early has the same effect. Money saved early will grow rapidly over time. It almost makes sense for a young person to borrow $10,000, put it into investments, and leave it alone. Sure you have to pay back the loan with interest, but it won't be anything like what it will earn after 40 years or so.

WHERE DO I BEGIN?

When you're planning a trip, you must know where you want to go, where you are now, the best route to take and what you'll do when you get there. It's no different when you're planning your financial future.

You must first know where you are financially. This may come as a surprise, a complete shock or a mild finding. If you're not depressed enough after finding you are in debt up to your eyeballs, think of how you can get out of this situation. Any trip starts at an origin. That's where you are right now.

Don't make plans about where you want to be in a certain amount of years until you do your homework and figure out how to dig yourself out of the hole you're in now. This part of the trip may take a good portion of your total plan. You must quit spending, save more and realize you can do whatever is required to get ahead. You must budget your next phase of the trip, stick to the budget and show a gain at the end of the first leg of the trip.

By now, you've read enough material to show you how to get out of the hole and start toward your goal. You must now think of where you want to go. To do this, you must also plan your path at the same time. Don't be unrealistic with your goals. It's good to be idealistic, but be realistic, too. Prepare a chart or graph showing dates or years across the bottom, and draw a line to gradually show an increase until a specific amount of dollars are met to achieve your goal. The line may look similar to a learning curve.

It'll be painful on the first leg of your journey, that of getting to the point at which you can start forward. So far, your trip has been down, not forward. There's nothing you can do about where you've been but regret it and hope for better days. When you see your-self gradually showing gains instead of losses, your self-esteem will increase, your attitude about money will change, and you'll learn a lesson about money and life.

Once you're moving forward, getting up to speed will be slow and steady. It takes a while and a lot of gut-wrenching sacrifices to climb out of that hole you're in. Once you're moving, it gets easier and easier to get up to speed.

It's hard to think about the future when payday is a week away and the checking account is empty. You can make money stretch further if you learn to manage it care-fully. You can stretch your money if you know what to do with the money, know where the money goes, know how to hang onto it longer, plan spending in advance and know and keep within your credit limits.

Your financial trip will be achieved in segments. If you're driving on a 2000-mile trip, you don't plan to drive it non-stop. You plan different lengths of drives, stopping to rest and plan the next leg of the journey. The same is true with financial trips. You must plan to take it in steps. It's a long and steady process.

If you and your family was in a covered wagon and on the Oregon trail, the trip would be smooth at times and very difficult at times. Hills, valleys, rivers and meadows would all represent different degrees of difficulty. The financial trip is the same, smooth sailing at times, and difficult problems at times.

If on such a trip, you had to unload items from the wagon and leave them behind to be able to continue your journey to your destination, what would you unload? Would you unload jewelry, food, clothing, etc.?

The same is true today. What would you unload to make the wagon lighter? Would it be clothing, jewelry, your boat, that second or third automobile, those trips out with the guys, the poker games or other things you consider non-essentials?

Now that you're on your way, you must keep a keen eye on the road ahead. Pitfalls may be everywhere, and the temptation to detour could sidetrack you or send you back where you came from. Only if you diligently do everything in your power to make the trip a successful one can you reach your goal.

I don't mean to burst your bubble, but I must tell you that the trip never ends. There's no time to stop and rest. Even when you begin to feel secure, don't let your guard down. When you reach your goal, go for another one and continue the trip.

Unless you inherit a fortune or win the lottery, everyone must make the trip.

Some will succeed, some will get part of the way, and some will miserably fail. Which will you be?

WORK AT BEING A CHEAPSKATE.

A cheapskate is said to be a shabby or miserly person. Hettie Green in the early 1900's lived on cold oatmeal, and left $95 million when she died in 1916. She was so stingy that her son had to have his leg amputated because of delays in finding a free clinic. She was too thrifty to heat her oatmeal.

A cheapjack is a person who deals in cheap merchandise. A cheapskate is the person who wants to do business with the cheapjack. To buy something at a cheap price means to buy below the going price or the real value.

You don't have to dress shabbily to be a miserly person. Neither do you have to be so miserly you ruin your life and those around you like Hettie Green did. Miserly people come in different degrees. Some act miserly when purchasing a car, home or furniture. Others go further down to purchasing clothing, household items, etc. Still others go to the extreme of spending entire days and nights trying to buy cheap, cheap, cheap.

When shopping for clothing, do you know where the clearance racks are in the stores in your town or nearby? You should. You should get to know the salespeople who work there so you can find out when certain items may go on clearance. Some items go on sale at certain times during the year. Keep notes of this.

You may want to sell some of your clothing to consignment shops. You can earn extra money to go toward the purchase of new clothing. Or you may want to buy from the same stores you sold to. The workers there may be able to set aside certain brand names or sizes before they go to the floor for sale.

Buy socks and underwear at the beginning of the school year for everyone in your family. They're always on sale at that time of the year, and you can stock up. To cut the hassle of pairing colors of socks, buy only black ones, the same kind and brand. They all match.

You can accessorize to save, too. One nave jacket can look great with a different scarf, pins, etc. If you buy only black, red and nave, they'll all match very well. While you're at it, buy only clothing that can be machine washed, saving dry cleaning cost.

Cheapskate recreation isn't that hard to find. Try local parks for cheap entertainment and events. They have art exhibits, music concerts and other sports events at times. Many are free or low in price.

The YMCA is another great place for the whole family. For a small fee, you can swim, roller skate, lift weights, watch movies, exercise, etc. Some have creative directors who provide quality entertainment for the whole family.

A $3 movie rental can save you mega bucks, and the stress of sitting in an overcrowded theater that's too hot or too cold. The popcorn at home may taste just as good, too.

Second hand sporting goods stores are spring up all over. So are used boot stores. You can get real bargains at these stores.

Years ago, I had over 400 women and about 25 men working for me. At Christmas time, they would complain about having to buy toys, etc. I mentioned to a few of them that I had a plan to save all of them a lot of time and money. I told them they should bring all their toys to a local park, display them, and swap with each other. Kids would get something they didn't have, and parents wouldn't spend a dime on them. They thought I'd lost my marbles. I still think it would work.

Instead of packing up the old jalopy with kids, suitcases and other stuff for a vacation, you may just want to stay at home for a week, cook out, have a great time and save money. You could even go camping. Everyone should enjoy this.

If you must fly on your vacation, always ask, "What is your cheapest rate and how do I qualify for it"? You may want to take a train on your next trip. This can be relaxing and fun. The cost is cheaper than plane trips. Just pack the necessities such as razors, shampoo, combs, etc. They can be expensive if you have to buy them later.

CREATIVE SURVIVAL FOR THE YOUNG AND STRUGGLING

Young people may not, and probably don't, know what a struggle it is to start a life of making and spending money. Most of them think anyone over thirty has it made and is living soft and easy. They have no idea how those people sacrificed to get where they are, and that's not soft and easy, either.

Some of those guys in the expensive suits may have collected and sold cans for money. They probably had to cut out the $3 a day for coffee that costs $750 annually. They even may have eaten lunch from a brown bag for a few years to get to where they are.

One way to cut costs is to co-op your lunches. Get a few of your friends to join you in an office-cooked lunch. Lunch for three can cost about the same as the bill for one lunch out of the office. Take turns cooking. It's like getting free meals. I do this and can tell you that it really works.

Watch the grocery store ads in your local newspaper. You don't need to always cut coupons to save money. These flyers have a lot of great deals. Stock up on them if they offer items that can be shelved or saved for a couple of weeks or so.

Always store a few items to eat in your desk drawer or file cabinet in case you forget to bring lunch one day. This saves an expensive trip to town and the hassle of eating out. I find peanut butter and crackers always come in handy.

Gather a few things from the cabinet, drive to the local park and have an enjoyable picnic with the wife and kids, or just the wife. Getting out of the house and away from the phone is a winning combination at times.

If you're young and furnishing that first apartment, take your time. Look for bargains. Go to thrift shops such as Salvation Army. You'll find lots of nice stuff that can be painted or just used as is. Buy cushions for those old chairs. Paint that old table to match your curtains or other items in the room. Recycle cans, etc. to save money for a special item you've had your eyes on. Not going into debt is more important than impressing your friends.

While you're looking for bargains for your first apartment, your neighbors may be almost giving theirs away at a yard sale down the street. Frequent these sales and spot that special thing you just have to have. Drive by the local college campus just after final exams to see what departing students are throwing out to keep from dragging it home. Sofas, refrigerators, etc. can even be found.

Clothing from a consignment shop will work quite well. You can even see designer labels there if that is a must for you. Used jeans can save you a bundle. Let it be known that you may be a frequent buyer there, and the price may be reduced for you.

In tough times, focus on friends, your future and having fun. One day, your time will come, and you'll be watching others follow the same trail as you have. Be patient and use your head to get through the rough times. You'll be surprised at what you can do without and will be stronger for it.

When your kids are going through the lean years just as you did, don't give them everything to make it easier for them. They need to learn to survive. Keep track of them and invite them over for dinner occasionally to help out.

CAN MY EX REALLY TRASH MY CREDIT?

If you think a divorce decree can save your credit, I've got some bad news for you. I can tell you from experience that a divorce decree, no matter what it says, doesn't void your obligations to a contract or credit card expenses.

My decree said the divorce was is if this marriage had never happened. Boy, was that a joke. I paid and paid and paid for years on things the decree said she would have to pay.

If your divorce decree says the ex will pay for that mobile home she was awarded in divorce court, and your name is one the contract, you can be held liable if she doesn't make the payments. Your credit can be trashed or ruined for a considerable length of time.

Your responsibility doesn't end once the divorce is final. Creditors don't care how property and bills are divided in divorce court. If both spouses signed a joint account, they both are responsible for paying it back.

A creditor can't be expected to abide with an agreement made after your agreement with him/her. The creditors may or may not let you know if payments are behind on an account. You could get blind-sided and not see it coming. If a home foreclosure happens and your name was on it, even though the ex got it in divorce court, you are responsible, too. Your credit reports will be blotted for seven years.

If you are both joint borrowers, you are both responsible for the debt. If one spouse is an authorized user on a credit account, he or she will not be liable for the debt. When the divorce occurs, do a check up to list any account or debt that you will be responsible for. Find out which accounts are still open. Close any accounts without balances as soon as possible to protect yourself. If you can't close it, remove authorized users from the account or simply try to freeze the account. A freeze will not allow you to use the account, but it will keep the other spouse from using it, too.

If your creditor allows you to do so, ask them to put a note in your file that you've divorced the spouse and tell them how you want the account to be handled. If they let you close the account, ask them to report to the credit bureaus that the account was closed per your request. Make it clear that you will not be responsible for further charges as of the day you call. Write down your conversation, including the time, day, contact names, etc.

Follow up with a letter recapping what you understand your agreement is with the creditor. Ask them to confirm in writing that they've taken the action you asked of them. In a couple of months, order your credit reports and make sure the accounts were handled properly. Contact the creditor if a closed account looks to be open or a frozen account has gotten bigger.

Make sure the bills are being paid. It takes months sometimes to finalize a divorce. Only one late payment can cause a problem. If you've already divorced and the ex is falling behind in the payments, you should send in payments yourself to protect your credit.

Foreclosure or repossession can destroy your credit rating. It happened to me when the ex was given the home in the decree and let it be repossessed before I knew what was happening. I couldn't buy anything like a car or home for seven years. I have never missed or been late in my life with a payment of any kind, but this happened to me.

If you can talk to the soon-to-be ex, ask for approval to sell the home or car and split the money left over. If the spouse will let you refinance the asset in his/her name only, go for it.

After she gets the gold mine and you get the shaft, continue to try to protect your credit. Gain Internet access to the accounts to keep a check on them to see if the ex is falling behind on the payments before your credit is ruined.

Be careful not to allow your name to be removed from the title if your name is still on the loan. You don't want to be responsible for the debt if you no longer own the asset.

Be careful, be civil with each other, and try to work out the details unless the other spouse is determined to be a horse's rump. Then you're in a no-win situation. Just hang onto your wallet with one hand and your rear end with the other. You could be in for a bumpy ride and a very bad run of luck.

FALLING INTO FINANCIAL QUICKSAND

Those of us old enough remember the black and white movies in which the Lone Ranger fell into quicksand, only to see Silver (his horse) toss him a rope and pull him from his potential doom. Even Roy Rogers, Tarzan and others fell into this pit of wet sand that would have pulled them under if not for the horse, a friend, a tree bent over the pit, or other items of rescue appeared to be there at the last moment.

Sometimes, they were up to their noses when rescue came. The odds are great that you never fell into quicksand, but there's another type of doom that can pull you under. That type is financial quicksand.

Most of you may be closer than you think to the quicksand. You walk around it every day of your lives. Some of you have fallen into it and were rescued. Some went under, never to recover.

In 1961, I was in New York and went on a bus tour of the city. I was especially sad to see skid row where people lay on the sidewalks and in back alleys, without food, a home, or even a dime on them. The tour guide explained that some of those people were teachers, professional people, and others who had lost everything through financial disaster of some kind.

I've always wondered how someone could get to this point in life. Today I see a multitude of people on the edge of financial disaster. The quicksand pit is very near, and some of them already have both legs in it.

When money trouble comes, it seems to come in clusters. The television breaks down, the washer quits, the stove won't heat, the computer dies, and other things happen at the same time. You may feel like the end of the world has come.

You can't bring in a priest to exorcise the debts. They'll be there until you confront them and do what is necessary to take care of them. There's no way to predict when this type of disaster will occur. You can plan to be ready when it does. You know appliances will break down, a water leak will happen, and that refrigerator you've had for twenty years will squeak to a halt.

Recently, my big screen television died. This happened at the same time I was giving the kitchen a makeover. Our sixteen-year old refrigerator was still running, but I managed to purchase a new television and modern refrigerator at the same dealer for a good discount. I sold the old refrigerator for $100. My power bill is down considerably due to the new refrigerator that is more energy efficient and the television that pulls a lot less wattage.

You may want to consider replacing those old appliances one at a time while they still can be sold for a fair amount. People who rent out houses are always looking for used appliances. When your car battery is four years old, replace it. This will save the frustration of being stranded in a parking lot or on the highway. Then you can look forward to four more years without worry again. If the television is ten years old, replace it for a newer model that uses less power and has a better picture. By timely replacement of some of these things, you won't worry about everything having to be replaced at once.

It's the accumulated stress of several things having to be replaced at once that is most bothersome. When looked at individually, it doesn't look so bad.

When you fall into the financial quicksand, you must act fast and smartly to recover. Waiting for Silver to rescue you isn't an option. You must grab for every bush, clump of grass or an overhanging limb you can manage to cling onto.

When this disaster hits, talk to a friend or family member about it. It won't remove your problem, but you'll feel more at ease about it. You must now take a deep breath and access the damage. It's time to be courageous and confront the problem head on.

This problem can seem overwhelming. You must know the total damage, the amount you have in reserve and what it will take to recover. The problem won't go away. You must quickly confront it, or you'll go under.

Using credit cards to recover will only transfer the problem from one pocket to the other. You'll now be in over your head. Some appliance stores will allow monthly payments without interest for a certain period of time. Some may now require payment for ninety days or so, giving you time to decide how to overcome the disaster.

Never borrow from a 401k to relieve the disaster that has occurred. This is the worst mistake you can make. If you don't have money in reserve to cover the costs involved, take on a part time job to ease the pain. Sell off some stuff you can do without. Have a garage sale or go to a flea market. You may be able to trade some things for a television, a refrigerator or a washing machine.

When a financial disaster hits, you may want to turn to relatives for a loan. But be sure to pay it back because the relative could have a disaster of his own.

You may ask, "Why me?" Financial disasters can happen to anyone at any time. We all have such times. If you haven't planned wisely and put aside funds for such a time, you feel even worse. Find out what it will cost to replace some of the things that will eventually break down. Put aside a certain amount weekly or monthly to cover the cost. You'll feel great about being able to pay cash for the replacements.

You must learn from disasters. You must take the opportunity to learn where you went wrong and what you must be ready for the next one. If you don't learn from your mistakes, you'll fall back into the financial quicksand.

Remember that the emergency fund is exactly that, an emergency fund. Don't go out and buy a new gun or coon dog with it. That new four-wheeler may look good to you, but if you take the emergency money to buy it, you've made a serious mistake. Saving an emergency fund may even teach you to save as you should, anyway.

When the water heater bursts and floods the house when you're away, you could have more than a water heater to replace. Floors and other items may also be damaged. If the water heater is very old, replace it with a more energy efficient one and take that worry out of your mind. You'll still have enough to worry about.

Keep a record of when you purchase appliances, have the house roofed or installed a car battery. Expect them to have to be replaced sometime. Set a time to replace them if they haven't been replaced before then. Save to replace them. This will relieve the stress of several disasters at once or a major one when you can least afford it.

If you think preventive maintenance is costly, try not doing it. You must educate yourself to the fact that disasters will happen, and they will happen to you. Don't blindly turn away from the possibility. You could find yourself trapped in financial quicksand, and nobody will be around to save you when you're sinking.

WHERE DID I GET ALL THIS STUFF?

Admit it, we've all got too much "stuff." We've got stuff we use every day, stuff we use once a month and stuff we don't see for ten years. We've got stuff in every room in our homes. We've got stuff in our automobiles. I have a change of clothing, golf clubs, tools, an umbrella, extra golf balls, oil, transmission fluid and duct tape in mine.

When we take a trip, we leave stuff at home, take stuff with us and buy new stuff before we depart. When going from the hotel to the beach, we take stuff with us and leave stuff in the room. We've got stuff everywhere.

The question we all should ask is, "Where and when did I get all this stuff?" It's everywhere. Look in your closet, the attic, the basement, under the bed and in the cabinets. Do you really need all that stuff to survive or even simply enjoy life?

The problem seems to be that we still accumulate stuff. It seems that every time we drive home, we've got stuff to unload. Sometimes I wonder where I'll put all that stuff.

It's said that we suffer from SDA, the Senseless Desire to Acquire. People acquire more today than years ago because we have the credit cards to make it easier. Before then, you needed "money" to buy things.

Sometimes I'll buy something that costs about $6.54 or so. My wife asks if I'm going to use a credit card. I tell her no, that I'm just going to "pay" for it. That may sound strange to you, but it's the way we seem to look at things now.

Most people have at least two beds in their home, some three or more. I'll bet you they have enough comforters, sheets, quilts, etc. to cover at least ten beds. These are things you wanted, not things you needed. You must decide the difference, want vs. need.

Look in your closets and see how many items of clothing you have. You could probably dress the Mormon Tabernacle Choir for an outing. It's not unusual for a lady to have thirty or forty dresses, seventeen pairs of shoes, eight jackets or coats and numerous other items. Some of them haven't been worn since aunt Sally had kids.

This kind of stuff is making us poor in the United States. Getting and spending is the source of personal financial trouble for most people. We think that whatever we own now needs to be replaced, upgraded or swapped.

If a young couple just got married and needed housekeeping things, most of us could totally outfit them with whatever they need, and we'd still have more than enough left. Every time I see people looking at clothing at a store, I wonder how many they already have and why they're even shopping. Ask if it is necessary, can you afford it and what is the cost of it.

The average home has increased about 40% in size since 1970, from 1500 square feet to 2300 square feet. That's even with the decline in the size of the average family. We're building larger homes with larger kitchens when most people eat out more than ever. More bedrooms are also being added. People with no children have four bedroom homes. Closets are now larger than my first living room.

We build bigger homes to accommodate more stuff. If you built a smaller home, would you try to keep all the stuff? Why? Bigger homes cost more in taxes, insurance, cooling bills, heating bills, mortgages, plus upkeep cost for the thing.

If you want that new boat, and you can afford it: can you afford the extra costs that associate with it? We give in to SDA and squander money on things that will only temporarily satisfy us.

When that bigger home is built, furnishing it how becomes a major problem. Do you let two bedrooms sit empty until you can afford to fill them? Do you hang sheets over the windows until you can afford designer curtains? Do you continue to drive the ten- year old car, hoping it'll hold out until you get a raise?

Keeping up with the Jones family can run you into bankruptcy. You don't pay Mr. Jones' debts, so don't try to keep up with his big car, his ten room house, his power boat, his registered dog, his 30 x 80 foot outbuilding, or his three carports.

We seem to pay dearly for convenience, immediacy and appearances. Building that huge home will cost a bundle. Buying a smaller, older one and investing in it over a period of a few years can save you a bundle. Instant gratification rules our lives. Long range plans seem far from our common sense.

Think before you spend. If you discover things you didn't know you had when looking in closets, garages, etc., sell them. My wife says if I haven't used it or worn it for two years, I don't need it. It's hard to argue with that logic, even if I am a man.

ARE REBATES A RIPOFF?

About half of all rebates on products go unclaimed. A lot of companies make the rules so tricky that the consumer won't bother to try to claim them.

The rebate theory seems very simple. You buy a product, mail in proof of purchase and the company will send you a check for the rebate. Rebate offers stimulate sales without reducing the price of the item.

The rebate business is tricky and full of potential for misunderstandings or possible fraud. It can be much harder than filling out an entry to Publishers Clearing House.]

The question of who issues the check is part of the problem. Confusion over where the rebate originates leaves us unable to target the problem.

Most rebates are offered from manufacturers, not retailers. The company that manages rebates is called a fulfillment company. They collect the rebate forms and proofs of purchase and tell the manufacturer what he owes. When the manufacturer pays up, the fulfillment company cuts the checks and mails them to the consumers. If the manufacturer is slow to pay the fulfillment company, the check is slow in coming.

A lot of problems come because the consumer doesn't or can't follow the complicated directions associated with the rebates.

The manufacturer has a vested interest in making the process difficult. The potential for fraud exists. It is said that $500 million is lost each year on fraudulent rebate claims. About half of rebates go unclaimed because customers lose the forms, throw away the UPC code or don't want to be bothered with filling out the rebate forms. As many as 800,000 claims a year are rejected because of improper filling, etc. This may amount to as much as $20 million.

You must know the redemption rules and follow them exactly. Don't buy just because the product offers a rebate. The price may be too high to start with. Read the fine print. The rebate periods do expire. Claiming the rebate online may save time if it is offered. They can be tracked in this way. No matter how redundant the request sounds for all sorts of data to go with the claim form, you must do it..

The reason the UPC cold is usually the one cut from the box is that this prevents you from filing for a rebate and then returning the product for a refund. Sometimes copying the UPC cold is allowed if there are multiple rebates available.

Make copies of any rebate forms submitted, including photocopies of receipts and UPC symbols. If dollars are involved, request a postal delivery confirmation. This will let you know the fulfillment house received your submission on time.

The average rebate takes six to eight weeks. Contact the manufacturer after the deadline passes to determine the status. If you're sure you did everything correctly, but still didn't get the rebate, complain with phone calls and written ones. Let your state attorney general office know if you suspect fraud. The Better Business Bureau also takes such complaints.

YOUR FINANCIAL SITUATION AFTER 40 YEARS OF WORKING

I've heard people brag about having $500, $1000, $25,000 or even $50,000 in the bank. But did they consider what part of their lifetime earnings this amounts to? The following chart shows the % of your lifetime earnings you've managed to hang onto. Let's assume a 3% annual pay increase and starting salary of $25,000 the first year you begin to work, with 40 years of work ahead of you. The first scenario assumes you accumulate what seems to be a large amount of money, $20,000. Scenario two shows you accumulated $400. Don't laugh. That's more than statistics show 60% of Americans will have when they retire, absolutely broke.

Year	life earnings	life savings	% saved
1	$25,000	$500	2%
2	$50,750	$1,000	2%
3	$77,273	$1,500	2%
4	$104,591	$2,000	2%
5	$132,728	$2,500	2%
6	$161,710	$3,000	2%
7	$191,562	$3,500	2%
8	$222,308	$4,000	2%
9	$253,978	$4,500	2%
10	$286,597	$5,000	2%
11	$320,195	$5,500	2%
12	$354,801	$6,000	2%
13	$390,445	$6,500	2%
14	$427,157	$7,000	2%
15	$464,973	$7,500	2%

16	$503,922	$8,000	2%
17	$544,040	$8,500	2%
18	$585,361	$9,000	2%
19	$627,922	$9,500	2%
20	$671,759	$10,000	1%
21	$716,912	$10,500	1%
22	$763,420	$11,000	1%
23	$811,322	$11,500	1%
24	$860,662	$12,000	1%
25	$911,482	$12,500	1%
26	$963,826	$13,000	1%
27	$1,017,741	$13,500	1%
28	$1,073,273	$14,000	1%
29	$1,130,471	$14,500	1%
30	$1,189,385	$15,000	1%
31	$1,250,067	$15,500	1%
32	$1,312,569	$16,000	1%
33	$1,376,946	$16,500	1%
34	$1,443,254	$17,000	1%
35	$1,511,552	$17,500	1%
36	$1,581,899	$18,000	1%
37	$1,654,356	$18,500	1%
38	$1,728,986	$19,000	1%
39	$1,805,856	$19,500	1%
40	$1,885,031	$20,000	1%

Let's look at what has happened here. By year 9 of work, you've earned ¼ million dollars and saved only $4,500. By year 16, you've earned ½ million dollars and saved $8,000. By year 27, you've earned $1 million and saved $13,500. By year 40 of work, you've earned almost $2 million and saved $20,000. That $20,000 sounds like a lot, doesn't it? After 40 years of work, your lifetime savings amounts to only 25% of what you earned that last year alone. I know I'm not counting interest earned on the money if you manage to invest it. You have managed to save only 1% of what you earned for 40 years work. You spent 99% of your earnings. And this scenario fits only a small group of people today.

Now, let's look at scenario two in which you work 40 years and end up with only $400, technically broke. Remember, that's where 60% of Americans will be.

Year	life earnings	life savings	% saved
1	$25,000	$10	0%
2	$50,750	$20	0%
3	$77,273	$30	0%
4	$104,591	$40	0%
5	$132,728	$50	0%
6	$161,710	$60	0%
7	$191,562	$70	0%
8	$222,308	$80	0%
9	$253,978	$90	0%
10	$286,597	$100	0%
11	$320,195	$110	0%
12	$354,801	$120	0%
13	$390,445	$130	0%
14	$427,158	$140	0%
15	$464,973	$150	0%
16	$503,922	$160	0%
17	$544,040	$170	0%
18	$585,361	$180	0%
19	$627,922	$190	0%
20	$671,759	$200	0%
21	$716,912	$210	0%
22	$763,420	$220	0%
23	$811,322	$230	0%
24	$860,662	$240	0%
25	$911,482	$250	0%
26	$963,826	$260	0%
27	$1,017,741	$270	0%
28	$1,073,273	$280	0%
29	$1,130,471	$290	0%
30	$1,189,385	$300	0%
31	$1,250,067	$310	0%
32	$1,312,569	$320	0%
33	$1,376,946	$330	0%
34	$1,443,254	$340	0%
35	$1,511,552	$350	0%
36	$1,581,899	$360	0%
37	$1,654,356	$370	0%
38	$1,728,986	$380	0%
39	$1,805,856	$390	0%
40	$1,885,031	$400	0%

These scenarios assume you keep the same job, with modest pay increases annually, and that you're never unemployed. You can see by now that you have pretty well spent your way to the poorhouse. I don't mean you move into a big white house on the hill and where you'll live off others. I mean you can't afford to quit work or may have to have a part time job to go with those small social security checks you must now try to live on. Even if you don't spend every dollar you earn, you could still wind up broke after a lifetime of work and accumulating "stuff" instead of planning and saving for the day you look forward to retirement.

DO YOU PLAN TO SPEND OR TO HAVE A SPENDING PLAN?

If you're an impulse buyer, you don't plan to spend. It may sound silly to you to have a spending plan, but you must plan certain expenses in order not to fall behind on the payments. You plan to pay your mortgage payment, your car payment, your utility bills, etc. You must also plan other expenses like replacing the aging washing machine, the water heater, the television, etc. If you don't have a plan, you won't have the funds to purchase these things when the time comes. And it will come when you least expect it.

It's said that the average person spends money about three times a day, one hundred times a month, twelve hundred times a year. Does that surprise you?

Look at an average day. You may spend for gasoline for the car, lunch, milk on the way home, dinner out, a soft drink from the vending machine, allowances for the kids, pick up the clothing from the dry cleaners, etc. It's amazing how much and how many times we reach into our pockets or purses and exchange our money for goods and services. The people who take our money also spend several times a day. Money is going around like it's on a merry-go-round.

When you plan for a vacation, you plan to spend on eats, car expenses, motel rooms, souvenirs, recreation and other activities and items. You should also plan on each day's expenses. When you go into that giant retail store to pick up three items, do you come out with seven or eight? You didn't plan on the others, right?

How much money do you keep in your pocket or purse on an average day? Do you have to drive through the bank line every other day to cash a check to meet the daily demands you've placed on yourself? Yes, I said you had placed them on yourself. You set your own financial destiny. Those bills you owe weren't sent to you without your action to create the expense.

When someone plans to go into a business of their own, they must write a business plan to show the type of business, the potential cost of setting it up, the forecasted income from the business and how you plan to operate the business. This plan is used by the lending institutions to decide if the new business is worth the risk of loaning money to get it up and going.

You must also write your personal spending plan. To do this you must know what your expenses will be, or should be. The way to do this is to enter the information onto a chart to show expenses individually for a certain period of time. You can then decide if you earn enough money to cover these expenses. If not, you've got work to do to cut expenses or increase your income. Use the following chart to post your budget expenses and also for actual expenses to track with the budget.

Copy the forms to use for actual vs. budget comparisons.

PLAN FOR SPENDING

Weekly	Monthly	Yearly	Goal

HOUSING

Mortgage or rent
_____

Home heating
_____

Electricity
_____

Water/sewage/garbage
_____

Home phone
_____

Cell phone/pager
_____

Property tax
_____

Repairs/cleaning
_____

Appliances/furniture

Floor/window covering

TRANSPORTATION
Car payment

Car payment

Fuel for cars

Repairs/ maintenance

License/registration

Parking/toll/taxi/bus

CLOTHING
Clothing

Dry clean/laundry

FOOD
Groceries

Lunch for work

School lunches

ENTERTAINMENT
Eating out

Trips/vacations

Television/cable tv

Music/sports/movies

Membership dues

_____

Other

_____

SAVINGS/INVESTMENTS
Bank/credit unions

_____

Savings plan at work

_____

IRA/Keogh/SEP

_____

Money market fund

_____

Emergency fund

_____

WEEKLY   MONTHLY   YEARLY   GOALS
HEALTH CARE
Doctor/dentist

_____

Medications

_____

Glasses/hearing aids

_____

Co-payments/deductibles

_____

FAMILY
Child care

_____

Personal allowance

_____

Child support

_____

Children allowance

_____

PERSONAL CARE
Cosmetics/toiletries

_____

Barger/beauty shop

Alcohol

Tobacco

Other

EDUCTION
Children's education

Hobby expense

Adult education

Newspapers

DONATIONS
Religious

Charitable

CREDIT PAYMENTS
Credit cards

Banks/credit unions

Student loan

Other

MISCELLANEOUS
Taxes/income-federal

Taxes/ income-state

Gifts/flowers

Pet care, food

Taxes/ social security

Other

TOTAL EXPENSES

NEVER TAKE A VACATION IN DEBTSVILLE.

It's said that 50% of Americans will take summer vacations, and about 75% will pay the bills with credit cards. The credit cards are more convenient and safer than cash to use, and they're accepted almost everywhere. The problem arises when you don't pay the full balance at the end of the next billing period. Most will take months or years to pay off the summer trip.

With extremely high rates on the cards, your little fling in Debtsville may cost you as much as if you had vacationed in Europe. More financial stress isn't exactly worth it, is it?

We work hard, and we deserve a vacation, right? If you mishandle it, you're going to have to work harder to pay for it. Maybe a trip to the local park or a night or two at a reasonable motel with a pool is in order. You deserve a vacation, but you don't deserve to pay for it for years and not be able to take the next one because of credit card debt.

The best way to plan for a vacation is to save the money for it, then obtain traveler's checks. If you see you are going to run out of such checks and money, come home. Don't even think about financing more time on a credit card. You should have planned better.

The average vacation cost could run from five to nine percent of our annual wages. Most people in America who do save will save only four percent of their wages. How can you justify such a vacation when you can't save enough to cover the cost of it?

Most think of vacations as an entitlement or a right. You do have responsibilities to go alone with those rights. Only half of us plan to pay the vacation cost total on our credit cards at the next billing cycle. You are truly in Debtsville.

At a card rate of 14%, a $2,700 vacation, when paying the minimum payment, will take 16.5 years to pay off, with $2,155 in interest alone.

Is it possible to take a vacation without ending up in the poorhouse? You must budget for a vacation. If you don't plan, you could actually vacation in Debtsville. Plan ahead and find good deals on motels, hotels, and airfare. But it doesn't do any good to plan and save on rooms and other things if you're only going to charge them on a credit card and pay the minimum payments on it.

If you are forced to save for that vacation, you may want to try garage sales, etc. to earn money. An automatic deposit from your check to a savings account could be a good way to save for the trip. It will also teach you the art of savings, too.

MONEY ADDICTION, GOOD OR BAD?

If you're addicted to money, does it mean you save every cent you can get your hands on, or does it mean you are addicted to spending all the money you can get your hands on?

All types of addictions can rule your lives. We can be addicted to money, power, possession, fame or spending. An addiction can be something we feel is essential to our sense of well-being or our wholeness. If you feel incomplete or unable to function with-out something, then you're addicted to that something. So, when you have a wealth habit, it may not mean you have so much money you are addicted. It may mean you must have money to spend, and spend and spend.

Would you be more comfortable in a 500 square foot apartment with very low rent or in a $200,000 home you can't afford? Would you be happier in a five-year-old car that is paid for or in a $40,000 car with $800 monthly payments?

Most people ride the financial roller coaster all their lives. They earn, save and spend over and over, with nothing left at the end. Earning is required to make a living. Spending and saving are optional, depending on our financial sense. I know people who earn much more than I earn who are so deep in debt they're miserable.

The advertising businesses prey on our emptiness feelings. They can help you fill that void in your life with stuff you may or may not need.

The key to overcoming an addiction is to develop the awareness that there is nothing missing in our lives. Money has nothing to do with our emotional capacity. I know that sounded strange. You say you must have money. That's correct to an extent. But you don't need piles of money to be happy. You need only to plan your life, work for it, and then be happy with what you have.

You can be addicted to alcohol, chocolate, bread, sex or a number of other things, but don't let an addiction to money ruin your life. Life is but a fleeting moment in time compared to infinity. Boy, that was deep, huh? Money, nor the lack of money, should not run your life and make you miserable.

There's nothing wrong with saving, and you should do it. To do without things that you need and that bring happiness while you hoard money isn't good. Neither is it good to spend every dime you earn as soon as you can do so. Working doesn't seem worth it when you realize you're addicted to money.

I'M SO BROKE----------------------

Okay, we've already read a lot about bills, money and going broke. Let's take a break from it and enjoy some jokes about being broke. We can still laugh even though we may be down to our last cent or let money test our sense.

I'm so broke I go to Kentucky Fried Chicken and lick other people's fingers.

I'm so broke, just to rub two nickels against each other I'd have to borrow one.

I'm so broke the bank asked for their calendar back.

If I stopped on a dime I'd probably owe it to someone.

I'm not broke, but I'm severely bent.

I'm so broke my girlfriend and I got married for the rice.

I'm so broke, if a trip around the world cost a nickel, I wouldn't have enough to leave the couch.

I'm so broke I just went to McDonald's and put a small fry on layaway.

If pickles were ten cents a truckload I couldn't buy a wart off a cucumber.

I'm so broke I can't pay attention.

I'm so broke, long distance companies don't even call me to switch.

A guy walked into our house, stepped on a cigarette and my mom yelled,

"Who turned off the heat?"

Someone saw me kicking a can down the street, and when asked what I was doing, I said, "Moving."

I'm so broke that when someone saw my mom walking down the street with one shoe, they said, "Hey, you lost a shoe." She said, "No, I found one."

We're so broke that if someone rings our doorbell I have to yell, "Ding dong!" out the window.

CAN WE REALLY JOKE ABOUT TAXES?

Some people say they are broke because of taxes. This may have some merit to it, you know. If you're a single taxpayer and earn $30,000 a year, you may pay $10,000 in taxes for car tax, social security and medicare tax, utilities tax, sales tax, federal tax, state tax, property tax and gasoline tax. That's 33% of your total year's earnings. If you're a higher wage earner, it gets even worse.

Let's take a few minutes to look at some good quotes about taxes, the government and Washington. Don't even dare think that we're paying taxes to a foreign government since the District of Columbia (Washington, DC) isn't technically a part of the United States. That excuse for not paying taxes will get you into tax-paid prison.

Most of us have enough money to pay our taxes. We just need money to make a living.

It takes the wool of twenty sheep and the hides of ten taxpayers to clothe one United States Soldier.

The income tax, the property tax, and the sales tax are an unbeatable combination. They get you going and coming. Add the inheritance tax and they get you after you're gone.

The only thing easier to skin than a banana is a taxpayer.

Pity the poor taxpayer who has the whole government on his payroll.

The sneakiest two words in the English language are "plus tax."

It's a weird world. The strong take away from the weak, the clever take away from the strong, and the government takes away from everybody.

A man listed the government as a dependent on his income tax return. The claim was disallowed because he wasn't contributing more than one half of his income toward its support.

There doesn't seem to be any justice. If you fill out an income tax return correctly, you go to the poorhouse. If you don't, you go to jail.

A tax refund is the next best thing to being shot at and missed.

There's no tax on brains—the take would be too small.

Some tax refunds are slower than a helicopter over a nudist colony.

The thing raised most abundantly in the United States if taxes.

Actually, we don't mind Uncle Sam's tax bite—if he didn't come back for dessert.

Only two kinds of people complain about excessive taxes—men and women.

Three cases where supply exceeds demand are: taxes, trouble and advice.

The trouble with today's taxes is that they keep your take-home pay from getting there.

A taxpayer recently sent the IRS twenty five cents with a note saying he understood that he could pay his taxes by the quarter.

The trouble with our foreign policy is that the enemy nations are living beyond our means.

The only people who don't have to pass the Civil Service exams to work for the govern-ment are taxpayers.

It's a lot easier to trim the taxpayer than to trim the budget.

When all is said and done, it's the politicians who say it and the taxpayers who do it.

The American taxpayer wouldn't object to free transportation for certain government officials if they'd go where we wish they would.

A deputy income tax collector in Washington was recently the victim of a holdup man who took all his money and stripped him to his underwear. Now he knows how we feel.

A taxpayer resents the fact that death and taxes don't come in that order.

With another tax hike, pants pockets will become unnecessary.

It' getting so your annual property tax is more than you paid for the home in the first place.

What about welfare for the taxpayer? He isn't faring so well these days, either.

There should be a special watch for the taxpayer—it wouldn't tick, just wring it's hands.

Taxpayers are always hoping for a break in the levy.

When taxpayers go broke or crazy, or both, they are taken care of by those who haven't gone yet.

A taxpayer might be referred to as a government worker with no vacations, no sick leaves, and no holidays.

Taxpayers are the casualties of the War on Poverty.

It might be well to bear in mind that when Uncle Sam plays Santa Claus, it's the tax-payer who holds the bag.

In the near future, Congress is expected to raise the legal limit on the taxpayer's patience.

We've had The New Deal and the Fair Deal. Some taxpayers are calling what we have now the Ordeal.

They say politics makes strange bedfellows, but it's the taxpayer who has the nightmare.

If Washington DC is the seat of the government, then the taxpayer is the pants pocket.

This talk about a "new source of revenue" simply means tapping the same old taxpayer in a brand new place.

There's nothing wrong with teenagers that becoming taxpayers won't cure.

A person doesn't realize how much he has to be thankful for until he has to pay taxes on it.

Responsibility for a considerable portion of the world's troubles rests upon two people of the past. One of them invented credit; the other taxes.

It was easier to tell the truth in George Washington's day. There were no income tax forms to fill out.

We often wondered why Uncle Sam wears such a tall hat, until he started passing it around to collect taxes.

Advice for vacationers: Don't overtax yourself. The government will do it for you.

Untold wealth is the wealth that is not reported on income tax returns.

Nowadays, when you miss a day's work, the government loses as much as you do.

Nowadays the world revolves on its taxes.

This is the day of youth, and they can have it. They'll age rapidly when taxpaying time starts.

It's getting harder and harder to support the government in the style to which it has become accustomed.

You have to admire the IRS. Any organization that makes that much money without advertising deserves respect.

Author Godfrey said, "I feel honored to pay taxes in America. The thing is I could feel just as honored at half the price."

Mark Twain said, no man's property is safe while Congress is in session.

Will Rogers said we do not seem able to check crime, so why not legalize it and then tax it out of business.

Income tax is the most equitable of all taxes. It gives everyone an equal chance at poverty.

When your ship finally comes in, how come the IRS is at the dock unloading it?

The difference in a taxidermist and a tax collector is that the taxidermist leaves the hide.

The IRS sure knows how to take our money. You really got to hand it to them.

The IRS is helping us with our errands this year. They are taking us to the cleaners.

Motto least likely to be seen in an IRS office: Money isn't everything.

Motto most likely to be seen in an IRS office: Success has its price.

Never put off till tomorrow what you can do today. If you do, there will probably be a higher tax on it.

On April 15 you can count your blessings, and then send them to Washington.

Ask the IRS agent this question: What did you do with all the money I gave you last year?

The new IRS office comes fully equipped. It even has a recovery room.

Birth control pills are deductible, but only if they don't work.

YOUR MORTGAGE COMPANY WON'T DARE TELL YOU THIS.

Mortgage payments can be one of the most painful things in the financial world to deal with. That home you have mortgaged is great to live in, but it comes with a lot of hidden and unhidden costs associated.

Most people sign a contract to pay for a certain amount each month for what seems like a thousand years and stick to that formula to pay for the home. Others try to find ways to pay off the mortgage quicker and more easily.

If you're one of the latter, rest assured there are ways to save thousands on your mortgage with painless and fast tips for the payoff of the mortgage.

If you are truly sincere in paying off that fat mortgage quicker, let's look into few ways this can be done. It doesn't mean you have to sell your truck, your boat or one of the kids to do it, either.

The reasons for paying off the mortgage quicker could be to pay less interest for the life of the mortgage, build equity faster, improve your credit rating, or it could be a form of forced savings for you.

Let's assume for calculations a $50,000 mortgage financed for 30 years at a 7% annual interest rate. Your payment would be about $332.65 for 360 months. Over the term of the loan, you would pay $69,755.52 in interest. This means you paid a total of $119,755.52 for the $50,000 loan. Good grief!

You can pay off the mortgage in ½ the time by simply doubling the principal pay-ment each month. An amortization will show you the monthly principal and interest due. The 360-month mortgage will now pay off in 181 months. The interest will be reduced from $69,755.52 to $35,051.88, a savings of $34,703.65. I know this sounds strange, but it will work. Just be diligent and stick to the program. You will have gone through only 3 or 4 cars by that time, not 6 or 8.

It's true that if you follow this plan, your payments will get larger and larger because the interest will be less and the principal more. Your last few payments may be almost twice the first one, but with patience, you can do it and save a bundle.

Another quick mortgage payoff is the 25% rule payoff. This method will save you $33,340 in interest, and the mortgage will be paid off in 17.3 years or 208 months.

Simply take 25% of the payment of $332.65. Apply the $83.16 to the principal each month. Your $332.65 payment becomes $415.81, but it is for 207 months, not 360. You cut 152 payments off your mortgage and save $33,340 in interest.

If the 25% method is not possible for you, simply determine what amount you can add to the principle each month, every month. You'll take years off the mortgage and save thousands of dollars. This won't break your budget, either.

If you're fat and happy paying the initial payment for 360 months, so be it. But if you truly want to save big bucks, try one of the above methods. When your mortgage is paid, plan to put the initial mortgage payment into a savings program for retirement. This way, you can survive after retirement.

HAVE YOU BEEN LEFT BEHIND?

Have you ever been left behind by a group of kids you were playing with? Were you left behind at other occasions or times? There's another more important way to get left behind.

The world is changing at a pace most of us can't keep up with. The things you learned years ago are important, but they won't get us through the day now. We must continue to learn and upgrade ourselves, especially in the economic matters that swamp and bewilder us today.

Too many people didn't get the math skills necessary to deal with economic problems today. Do you really know how to work up a budget? Do you know how to figure what to do with stock investments if you're lucky enough to have the problem?

I recently saw a math test in our local newspaper. The test was from an eighth grade class about 100 years ago. It said that most people today couldn't pass the test. Just for fun, ask a teacher for a current eighth grade math test. Take the test and see how you stack up with the kids today. You'll probably find you've been left behind in this area.

Paying taxes, calculating your bills, deciding which investments are best, etc. bewilder most of us today. We seem to be getting further and further behind. We now must play catch-up in order to make every day decisions about our financial lives. More and more experts are charging people to help them in financial matters.

If you didn't finish high school, you're definitely behind. Even if you did, you're probably behind. I've met a lot of college kids who can't seem to grasp the numbers racket today. At best, it's a game in which you can go broke, get rich or simply not play.

The longer you go without trying to play catch-up, the harder it is to perform in this world of numbers and decision making. You should take classes or do whatever you can to catch up.

I was fifty years old before I touched a computer. I now make a living on one. Most people over fifty are computer illiterate. Today, a computer is a life saver. If you go to a large library to check out a book, you may not go through the flip cards in a little drawer to find the location of a book. You may see a circle of computers at which you must put in the name of the book or the author.

Days have long passed since I used the Commodore 64 to play lunar landing games. You now have a computer with gigaflops of power, and you must first learn where to turn the monster on. Instructions are mind-boggling for most of us. Just getting into the thing to get information requires a degree in computerology.

Don't be ashamed to admit you've been left behind in this numbers world. Just do something about it by upgrading yourself. Even if you must get help from a child, do it.

As a child, we learned a lot from our parents. Today, our kids can teach us a lot. Look at what they're studying in school. It's not the same thing you saw. Even if it was, it takes a different route to get to the answer.

If you're falling for those lines from super salesmen and saleswomen because you simply cannot comprehend what they're saying or showing you, take a break, study, and get into the game. Sometimes you only have to sound like you know what you're talking about.

When I bought my first computer, I read about a few things I should ask for and know before my trip to the smiling young guy who delights in making a fool of me. Now that computer won't even serve the minimum requirements to get on the web or run other programs I need. I had to upgrade to a super-dooper computer that holds millions of bits of information, even if I don't know that much.

Don't get left behind. Read, study, attend a class or whatever it takes to keep up. You're going to need it. The world is changing much faster that we can imagine, and only part of us will be able to survive financially in it.

BEWARE OF THOSE LOW INTEREST CREDIT CARD TRANSFERS.

We all get those offers from credit card companies to transfer your balances to their card at a low rate. You can actually see the rate on the envelope before you open it. The terms are in fine print and very tricky. You'll get that low rate only if your credit report is good. It's not automatic. Be very careful before answering such mailings.

People are trying to find ways to reduce their debt load. If you pay less than the full amount due on a credit card at the payment due date, you're already in trouble. If you pay only the minimum payment, you're in serious trouble.

These introductory low rates may only last five to nine months, if you qualify for one of them. They are teaser rates to get you to transfer your debt to their card.

Even if you're an ideal card customer and qualify for one of these low rate transfers, one slip-up is all it takes for the issuer to jack up the interest rate. One late payment could replace that 0% rate with a 19% rate immediately.

Some card companies reward you for transferring balances to their low rates for any new purchase made on the card. Some will offer this rate for purchases for the next six months. Some will charge a fixed rate on balance transfers until the balance is paid off.

Be very wary about these deals. The penalties could be severe on some of these low rate cards. Some companies charge a transaction fee for the privilege of transferring a balance to their card.

Some offer a low 3% rate, then charge you a 4% fee on a $1,000 balance, resulting in a transaction fee of $40. These fees are charged to you as soon as the balance is trans-ferred onto the card.

It could take up to four weeks to finalize the transfer, so be sure to make at least minimum payments on the old card during this time.

After transferring to a low rate card, be sure to close off old credit lines. You don't want to be tempted to continue charging on the old card, too. Soon, both cards will show large balances, and you're in over your head.

Not everyone will qualify for the transfer at the low rate promised. The very tiny print at the end of the card offer explains this. It's said that the big print giveth and the small print taketh away.

After you've qualified for the new low rate and the transfer is made, your payments will be lower. If you could save the difference, that would make a nice emergency fund. But it would be better to pay more than the minimum payments on the card to truly reduce your debt and pay off the account quicker. Your goal should be to eliminate credit card debt. Pay all possible on the balance.

You also need to adjust your spending habits to avoid running up big balances again. This means to live within your means. You should limit card purchases to emergencies or for purchases that you can pay off in 90 days or less.

So, when you get all those low interest transfer offers, unless you can handle it and not go deeper into debt, tear them up and pay on the old card quicker. Of course, not using the old card is even a better alternative.

When you charge and don't pay the due amount in full, you're financing that expense just like you financed your home. It is now a liability because what you pay for it is much more than it is worth. You net worth just go smaller.

WHY DO YOU BORROW, AND FOR WHAT?

We borrow for every reason under the sun. We borrow to purchase a home, a car, furniture, a vacation, clothing, a kitchen make over, Christmas, etc.

To be honest, there's only one reason to borrow money if you're financial spending and savings habits are good ones. That's for a home. To borrow for anything else is not a very good idea. The home increases in value, but other things just depreciate and fade away.

I know. You say you have to borrow for educational expenses, a car or even new furniture. The car is a maybe. Not all of us are mindful enough to save for a new car. But to borrow for appliances, furniture, educational expenses, etc. is a direct result of poor planning.

If you know you must replace the refrigerator, the stove, the living room furniture, etc., set up a plan to save for them. You're going to have to pay for them anyway. So, why pay for them and also pay interest on them?

Decisions abut when and why to borrow may have a bigger impact on your overall wealth than any other decision you'll have to make. Borrowing is usually an immediate impulse to have something or do something. We don't think of the long-term debt associated with borrowing.

You wouldn't hit your foot with a hammer before running a race. By borrowing money and paying interest, you are decreasing your total wealth to accomplish a goal or buy something. If that asset you borrow to buy declines in value, you've put yourself deeper in debt and reduced your total wealth. You've created a liability.

Do you think you make financial decisions in a rational way? It's assumed that every-one's goal is to increase his wealth. If you're a rational person, you'll examine every financial decision to see how it affects your wealth over a long term, not a short one.

Most people look at financial matters as a short-term decision, not a long-term one that can affect your total wealth. If you obtain a loan and pay interest on it, the money has to come from somewhere. Do you take it from your retirement account, your vacation account or your emergency fund?

If you pay minimum payments on a credit card balance, you may be paying for that nice dinner 30 years after you've digested the food. Most credit cards demand a minimum payment of 2% to 3% of the balance. On a $5,000 balance, you may pay $150 a month minimum. If your payment is $150 minimum, pay $20 and stop spending on the card. The balance will disappear faster and you'll learn financial management.

A home mortgage is one loan that still provides a tax deduction for interest. This makes the real cost of a mortgage less than that for other debts. If you're in a 27% tax bracket, the government pays 27% of your interest. That means you pay $13,500 a year in mortgage interest, and the real cost to you is only $9,450.

If your mortgage interest rate is 8%, you pay only 73% of that, or 5.84% interest rate. If inflation is at 2%, your real interest rate would be 5.84% less 2%, or 3.84%.

Other than borrowing for a home, everything else should come from an emergency fund or from short and long term savings.

So you should set up short and long term goals, set aside money for future purchases and expenses, and maintain as high net worth as possible, avoiding high interest payments.

PMI? IS IT AN ILLNESS, A DISEASE OR JUST UNNECESSARY?

If you're paying a mortgage payment, and you've been paying on it for years, this is very important to you.

PMI, private mortgage insurance, is insurance the buyer pays for, but it protects the lender's interest. Conventional loans require at least a 20% down payment. That much money can push most over the edge, out of reach of home ownership. PMI allows you to get a mortgage with a smaller down payment.

Then you must also pay PMI to protect the lender from non-payment of the loan payments. This makes it easier for you to get a loan, but your payments will be bigger, and you'll owe PMI until your equity in the home is at the 20% level.

While it is added to your monthly payment, PMI allows you to get that home of your dreams. On a $100,000 mortgage at 7% for 30 years, the monthly payment would be about $665. PMI could add about $43 more to that payment.

PMI is no longer required when you've made enough payments to bring the home equity to the 20% level. Of course, you may also want to convince by appraisal that the home has increased in value enough to bring the equity above 20%.

The Homeowners Protection Act requires that the lender automatically cancel PMI when you have 22% equity in the home if your payment history is good. This law applies only to conventional mortgages after July 29, 1999. The law does not apply to FHA and VA loans. The FHA mortgage insurance program extends for the life of the loan.

If your conventional loan is an old one, you may be paying unnecessary PMI and not know it. It's the responsibility of the homeowner to notify the lender when their equity surpasses 20%. A lot of people have paid the PMI for years too long.

Building up equity in the first years can be very slow. If you get a 30 year mortgage at 8% and pay only 3% down, it would take 12.7 years of payments to get to the 20% loan-to-value ratio.

AT the appreciated rate of 3% or 4% a year on the home, your 20% equity time could come quicker than you realize. But you still must notify the lender.

If you've made additional principal payments, you should contact the loan officer to ask for the PMI to be cancelled. The appraisal will cost a few hundred dollars, but it could save you a lot of money in the long run.

Remember, PMI on newer mortgages will automatically cancel, but that won't happen on pre-1999 mortgages. Pay attention to the monthly PMI payment and the market value of your home. Canceling PMI early could save a lot of money.

WARNING SIGNS YOU ARE IN FINANCIAL DECAY

Most people think the first warning sign of financial problems is that they're broke. The real signs started long before that event. Some of the following warning signs may sound funny, but they probably apply to some of you.

Warning signs of financial trouble:
You pull a roll of film from your camera that has been in there for months and go straight to the 1 hour processing center.

You have to wait until payday to develop the pictures you took with your $500 camera.

You buy a car worth $35,000 and worry about gas prices.

Your minimum monthly payments on your credit card balances combined is more than your rent or mortgage payment.

You think paying your Discover card bill with your Visa card and your Visa card bill with your Discover card means you won't ever have to write a check.

You buy more food before you have eaten the food you bought last week.

You get upset when assessed a late fee after you failed to pay your bill on time.

You actually pay more in finance charges than you give to God's work.

Your fines from the library or video store are more than you paid for the rent.

The electric company calls you personally to cut back on usage during peak electrical usage in your community.

You think a Casino will be your source of retirement money.

You think your 3% raise means you can spend 3% more, when you actually take home only 65% of it, or 1.95% after deductions.

Your wife cuts your hair to save money so you can buy a $150 tracking collar for your coon dog.

You drive 26 miles round trip to the bank to cash a $5 check.

You buy 2 apples for a quarter instead of getting them for ten cents each.

You buy the cheapest toilet paper you can find and leave a leaking toilet running for months.

You ask your kids for part of their allowance so you can have gas money to go to work.

You pay $37 for your and your spouse to go to a movie and eat a hamburger to hold down the cost of going out.

You try to get the barber to reduce his price because you are half bald.

You spend your entire tax refund on something you would not have bought if you had not received a refund.

Your neighbor asks you to go fishing with him and you can't afford a license.

Your children offer you money to help buy groceries.

The bank calls you to tell you they can't afford to pay postage on your monthly statement because you have only $2.50 in their bank.

You have to park outside the baseball park and peek through the fence to see the game.

You have to vomit to feed your dog.

HOW MUCH SPACE DO YOU NEED?

The average size home today is probably about 2,000 square feet. Have you thought about how big that is? That's about 45 x 45 feet square.

If you lie down on the floor, you will probably require about 10 square feet at most. The average home is 200 times that big. I know it takes space for the 17 square foot television, the 28 square foot refrigerator/freezer and at least 42 square feet for the king size bed.

If we didn't have so much stuff, we wouldn't need so much space. I've seen a man and wife only living in a three-story house with four chimneys and a basement. There must be some rooms they haven't seen in weeks or months. Someone could sneak in and live in the home for months before being noticed.

I cut and sold firewood when I was a young man. I delivered a load to a prominent couple's home in a very expensive neighborhood. When I went to the door, I noticed two doors about 12 feet high and 4 feet wide, with a large knocker on one door. I raised and lowered the knocker to hear a boom, boom. It sounded like civil war cannons. The lady told me to go to the back of the house to unload the firewood.

At the rear of the home, I saw an outside fireplace for cooking. It must have been about 10 feet wide and thirty feet high. The same fireplace extended into the home. I thought I would surely be making a trip a day there, as much wood as this monster would burn.

Inside the home, in the basement, was the Red Dog Saloon. I mean a saloon as large as the Long Branch run by Miss Kitty on Gunsmoke. The farther down the street you went, the bigger and more expensive the homes. This one was the last house on the street.

What could a couple in the 50's want with such a home? It must have been a pride thing. They could pass each other in the house without seeing each other.

With the price of a home ranging from $40 to $100 a square foot, it's easy to see how so many people get in over their heads. The cost of insurance, taxes and upkeep will be in direct proportion to the square footage.

If you buy such a large home, you certainly don't want cheap furnishings in it. The bridge club may be offended.

How much space do you really need. My wife says I was born 150 years too late, that I should have been born in the early 1800's. She's probably right. I could live in a one-room home with a curtain pulled across to divide the bedroom from the rest of it.

I honestly believe a single person, and maybe a couple, could live in a 20 x 20 foot home, with the kitchen in one corner, a bathroom in another, a bed in another and a television in a strategic spot.

Put me in a forest, with a cabin with a porch, a chimney, an outhouse, a solar cooker, etc. and I wouldn't care who the president was. I told my wife I wouldn't mind living in the northwest woods, 50 miles from a small town, and have to get up each morning and scrape the bird poop off the windows to see outside.

It's time to downsize, people. It's time to reassess our needs and reassess our wants. We deliberately and non-deliberately spend too much on too much stuff. Our homes are large to hold all our stuff. Our carports are full of stuff, causing the car to sit outside.

It's time to get real. As time goes on, people will have less money sense and will depend on having more to be happy. More won't make you happier, just more in debt, causing you to have to run a job you don't like and can't possibly loosen yourself from because of your debts you've created.

FULL TIME MOTOR HOME LIVING

If you're fortunate enough to have worked and saved money, or have a 401k nest egg, the following may be appealing to you.

Living within our means and getting by doesn't mean just during the early years of working. After you're into the September or October of life, financial planning is just as serious and necessary, sometimes more important.

If the cost of maintaining the old family homestead and paying high utility bills concerns you, think about an alternative.

If your home is paid for, you may want to look into selling it for a very nice motor home. I know you are thinking I've lost my mind, but keep yours open and carefully explore the alternatives.

With home prices what they are, you may be surprised to know that you can buy a 32' motor home for about $60,000 or so. You can probably sell the home for enough to buy one of these traveling hotels and have enough to set up for a fun and adventuresome time ahead.

I'm not talking about hitting the road and driving every day. I'm talking about doing your research on camp sites and motor home parks. You drive the home to a nice lot and park it for an extended time, maybe months or a year or so.

Parking sites may cost from $16 and upward a day. The good news is that that price includes all hook-ups. Power, water, gas, etc. is included in the price. How much do you now pay for utilities? With a $20 daily hook-up, your total cost is 600 a month. You won't be paying property taxes, city taxes, etc. The cost will be the same or close to the same for all seasons, maybe a little more in summer.

Do the math. Calculate your current expenses of owning a home and compare it with full time at a motor home site and paying the same every day.

Be careful to select a site close to restaurants, grocery stores, entertainment, etc. Location could mean a good stay or a bad one.

When you're tired of the location you've been parked in for a few months, simply unhook and drive a while to find a new one. This type of variety could make life less boring and stressful.

Have you looked in one of these motor homes? They aren't trailers, anymore. They have microwaves, big refrigerators, king size beds, a plazma television, large showers, a dining area, etc. Some use hydraulics to extend certain areas outward as much as four feet or so. They look like swanky hotel rooms inside. Instead of paying $100 or more a night for a hotel room, live in a larger, nicer one full time for a lot less money.

You may find a nice parking site close to a national park, on the outskirts of a nice town or city or by a lake with beautiful scenery. The possibilities are endless.

On the road between sites, some motor home owners are finding secure parking at places like Wal-Mart or Kmart. You should first contact the store manager and part in the far end of the parking lot if given permission. Most super stores have security around, which won't hurt. Store managers see you as potential customers, too.

Overnight parking at a busy truck stop is possible, too. There, you'll find good food and other people around. Your business would also be appreciated when you eat or buy fuel there.

Insurance on the motor home will be more than on a car, so be sure to shop around for knowledgeable agents about motor homes. Get the right deductible and don't skimp on liability coverage.

When I tell my wife I'm going to buy a motor home when I retire and hit the road, she just tells me to enjoy my trip and come back safe. I've still got a few years to break her in to the possibility of some travel and full time living in a motor home. It sounds exciting, doesn't it?

TIME IS MONEY.

You've all heard the quote, "time is money." That's truer than you may want to admit. When it comes to saving and investing, it's usually safe to say that the longer you invest your money the more you'll have when you need it. You may ask how this is possible.

It's possible because of the "Rule of 72." You can divide 72 by the % interest you are getting on your savings or other investment to find out how long it takes for your money to double in value.

If your interest rate is 5%, 72 divided by 5=14.4 years for the money to double. If the interest rate is 5%, 72 divided by 6=12 years for the money to double. An investment earning 12% interest would double in 6 years. If you routinely add to the account, it will double quicker.

The definition of saving is: amount of money put away for later use. If you see an item for $100 and pay for it, you've made no investment except in an item that will depreciate over time. If you save the $100, interest will be earned over time to allow you to have more to spend later.

To save, we must economize. This means we must get the most from our resources. To save money, you have to stop spending so much.

To save, you must have an incentive to do so. It may be a car, a new coat, a television or maybe a vacation. The incentive has to be strong enough to push you to save for it.

We hear about government deficits. You probably have the same such deficit in your home. A deficit occurs when expenditures exceed income. Surely you don't have that problem, do you? Most families do, week after week for most of their lives. To avoid a deficit, your income must exceed your expenses. This takes patience and will power. Most people think that if they make more, they must spend more. To save part of your check every payday is a must if you will survive. We can't crank up the mint to make us more money like the government does.

Have you ever thought of making a profit when you don't own a business? The truth is that you do run and own a business. It's called a family. If you don't make a profit and have money to save, you have a loss, not a profit. It works on the same principal as owning a business.

Risk management minimizes possible financial loss by identifying consequences of a loss, and creating a risk management plan for actual losses and their consequences financially. Boy, that's deep, huh? If you're seeing a loss in your financial life, you must identify the location or cause of the loss and stop it before bankruptcy or other action is necessary. To identify this loss, you must admit it to yourself and your family.

You practice risk management every day. Some are a lot better at it than others. You're taking a risk of increasing or decreasing your assets every day.

Time is truly money. Money is earned over time, and it is invested over time to grow and pay you back for good risk management. Take advantage of it.

MONETARY STRESS WITHIN THE FAMILY

His holiness the Dalai Lama said, "True compassion is not just an emotional response, but a firm commitment founded on reason. Therefore, a truly compassionate attitude toward others does not change, even if they behave negatively. Through universal altruism, you develop a feeling of responsibility for others: the wish to help them actively overcome their problems."

People sometimes bring attitudes about money that we forged long ago into a new relationship. It's important to understand the real monetary issues in a relationship. We must learn to express our feelings, to communicate properly, to actively listen to our partner and to create a common goal to accomplish.

In a new relationship, we must forget or let go of our money habits in the past. We must realize there is a new future now, and we must work within the present.

Not dealing with the problems arising from our attitude toward money is actually dealing with it badly. We must work on facts, not problems in a past relationship.

Most family money problems are a result of a disagreement of how to spend the money or maybe dealing with the fact that there isn't enough money to go around.

You must decide what is most important to make the relationship work. If the relationship is more important than the excuses we carry around, you must make a concerted effort to make a change in the way you behave about monetary problems.

I know couples that actually have separate bank accounts and saving accounts. I suspect the wife didn't want to spend on the coon dog or the four-wheeler or the new gun. Or maybe the husband doesn't want to be a part of buying new clothing every week. Either way, these people aren't communicating. Selfishness and greed can destroy a relationship.

Some fear being controlled by someone else, so they want to be in control of their expenses, etc. You must sit down with the other person and list all bills, wants and needs. Then decide which have to go and which stays. It won't hurt either to give in at times. It makes the relationship stronger.

At times you might complain about the problem so much that you start identifying with the problem, and you become the problem itself. If you don't develop a positive attitude about money, your negative attitude will keep you in the same old position.

Negative or passive-aggression can create a negative attitude that is hard to overcome. The constant criticizing of others will ruin a marriage or relationship.

Some people will demand that they are right when making decisions about money. They fail to consider the fact that they may be 50% wrong or even 100% wrong. As a husband, I know that at times you must decide if you want to be right or be loved. Giving in doesn't make you less of a man or a woman. It simply reduces the stress of the monetary problem within the home.

If you know there is a solution to a money problem, you shouldn't worry about it. If you know that there is no solution, why worry about it? Voltaire said that 90% of his life he spend worrying about problems and disasters that never materialized.

Let's face it. You are not going to change your partner. A spending partner will be a spending partner until you work it out together. Concessions will have to be made, maybe more on one part than another, but made for sure. If you have to give a little to achieve the goal, so be it.

I WASN'T PLANNING TO SPEND THAT MUCH.

We've heard the expression that you didn't plan to spend that much. Of course, the statement is usually said "after" too much has been spent.

Jerry asks his wife, Judy, what she wants for their thirtieth anniversary. "Would you like a new mink coat?" Judy said, "Not really." "How about a new Mercedes?" She said, "No." "What about a new vacation home in the country?" She said, "No thanks." "Well, what do you want?" Judy said, "I'd like a divorce." Jerry said, "I wasn't planning to spend that much."

One guy, down on his luck, said, "If I had a dollar bill, it would die from loneliness." It's easy to make jokes about being jobless or broke, or just getting through financially hard times, but it's really no laughing matter if it happens to you.

Most people will experience a financial upset in their lives through a job loss, divorce, medical problems, etc. But even being frugal doesn't mean you can create money from nothing. If you're on the verge of being homeless, every cent you can save won't be enough to pay the mortgage if your income isn't enough to cover it. You're in deep trouble when your utilities are cut off, the car is being repossessed or if you can't afford enough groceries. At this point, you must get help.

If you're on welfare, you could starve while waiting for the food stamps, but the situation is very desperate. Even the government will get into emergency funds to help the problem. Contact the Salvation Army or other charitable organizations for help. Many churches will have outreach programs to help.

Then you must do all possible to help yourself. Within the law, do whatever is available to give a little relief. Sell whatever you can. Offer to run errand, mow yards, baby sit, or even make a few things to sell. Sell excess furniture. Sell kitchen things you won't need soon. You certainly won't need them if you lose your home.

Don't spend anything you don't absolutely have to. Don't pay a dollar for a cup of coffee. Make a dollar and put it aside until you can buy a pound of coffee. Buy just enough gas to get you around. Don't tie up money for food. Cut down on household expenses. Take shorter showers. Sweep instead of vacuuming.

If times get hard enough, go to the grocery store and ask for things the store is throwing out. Get all the samples they have to offer. Eat less expensive foods. Peanut butter has a lot of the things we need in our diets.

Don't get down. Keep your head up. Remember that nothing is forever, not even being broke. You must make the most of everything, pull yourself up and get back on the road to recovery.

BUT I CAN'T DO WITHOUT THOSE THINGS.

Do you have one, tow, three or more cell phones? Do you have call-waiting, call-forwarding, three-way calling, speed calling, hi tech phones, etc.? Do you really need all that stuff? It's no free, you know.

Do you have a 26-horsepower riding mower for your teeny little lawn? Does it also have a grass catcher and a pull-behind trailer? Did you have to build or buy an outbuilding to put the thing in? You can do the same job with a 14 horsepower mower that used much less fuel. You don't need to keep up with the Jones family on this one. They're probably still paying for theirs on a credit card.

Does your pickup truck have oversized tires, running lights, running boards, twenty five extra lights, a roll bar, an optional set of amplifiers, chrome wheels, etc.? Some guys need a ladder to get into the thing. It seems some guys never forget when they would put down a small plastic or wooden truck or tractor toy and drag it across the dirt and say, "Vroom, vroom."

Could you cook a four-course meal for the Mormon tabernacle Choir on your gas grill all at once? I've seen grills that cost more than the cost of a steak every day for seven months. I think a whole pig would fit on some of them. It must be a status thing. You know, "Mine is bigger than yours."

Does your dog have a $150 tracking collar on him? Does it cost $100 a month to feed him? Does it require a miner's hat and a $300 dog box in the rear of the pickup? That little desire to hunt isn't picking up your gun and going out anymore, is it?

I know you've got a computer. But, do you need one that dims the lights when you turn it on or shorts out the cable television line or causes low-flying planes to fall 5,000 feet when you turn it on? You don't need one with sixteen gigaflops of memory that will hold the pentagon's files. Then, you only play games on it or explore the intranet. How much is enough?

My son has three children, and they're all into sports and camping. Recently, I set up a four-day tent camping trip for them. I'm not telling this story to criticize him, only to show the results of such a journey.

He saw a pop-up camper for sale, looked at it and just had to have it. After getting a deal on it, he purchased it. Then came costs associated with having it. A daily cost of at least $14 for a parking site, extra money for gas for the trip and supplies necessary add up to money he can't afford to spend. But, he has the camper, and using it will justify the cost, I guess.

This sounds like the guy who bought western jeans, had to have boots, hats, shirts and a new belt. If he had not bought the $40 jeans, he wouldn't have spent another $177 for accessories.

HONEY, I'VE GOT TO GO TO THE STORE.

You've heard the story. You've probably done it yourself. It's 8 pm and you discover you need milk for breakfast. The nearest store is six miles away. You put your shirt on, jump into your car or truck, drive twelve miles and pay $3.50 for a gallon of milk. Or did you? What you actually paid was $3.50 for the milk + $.72 for gas + $1.75 for the car depreciation for tires and other costs. That's $5.97 for a gallon of milk, not including your time.

If you have a convenience store in the town in which you work, you may get the milk for as little as $2.75 a gallon. Some milk cards will give you a free gallon for every sixteen gallons you buy. That brings the cost down to $2.59. While you're there, pick up bread and gas up the car. The gas will probably be cheaper than at other stations. Now you won't have to fuss at the spouse about who forgot the milk, missing the last thirty minutes of your favorite television show, cause all the neighbors to wonder why you're going out so late or run over the cat on the way out. Assuming your family drinks 75 gallons of milk a year, you'd save $194. That would pay for 6-7 rounds of golf, right?

Of course, there are other particular reasons to have to go back to the store at night. If you're a chocoholic like me, I'm sure you've done this. One night I got up from my recliner at 9:15 and drove down the mountain five miles away for a chocolate bar. If you keep a bag of such morsels in the cabinet, you probably won't want one. Just knowing it's there helps.

My wife has an add-on grocery list. In between weekly grocery shopping trips, we simply add anything we'll need before the next weekly trip to the list. We always keep a spare of toothpaste, deodorant, shampoo, soap, toilet paper, shave cream, etc. When the spare is opened, it goes on the add-on list. This prevents those sudden urges to use your time and money to go to the store one stormy night.

Wait, there's more cost to add. While you're at the store on one of those unnecessary trips, you'll also see something else you want. This stuff is packed at the check out counter, and you'll have to pay a hefty price for it.

Plan smarter trips to the store by stopping by on your way home from work. You'll hear that sound of loose change in your pocket and learn something good to pass onto your kids. Remember, the kids are trying to develop life long habits from someone who can't remember to get milk or bread on the way home.

IT'S EASY. WE'LL JUST REFINANCE UNTIL WE DIE.

You've all seen those stupid television commercials where the lady says she re-financed her car, her washing machine, credit card balances, house and other things to arrive at a monthly payment $300 less than the total of all those bills before refinancing. Then, she says that's the way she got that nice new swimming pool or that she can finally take that long-awaited vacation now.

This type of behavior qualifies as "mental accounting." What is mental accounting? Take this scenario. A guy drives downtown to purchase a window fan. The clerk says it will cost $75. The guy knows that two miles down the road, the same fan costs $50, a savings of $25. Will he drive a few minutes top save the $25? He probably will. The same guy goes to purchase a television. The set costs $375. About two miles away, the same set is selling for $350, a savings of $25. Will he drive two more miles to save the $25? He probably won't because the savings on the television is a smaller % of the price than on the fan. The fan saved 33%. The television meant only a savings of 7%. Hey, folks, $25 is $25, no matter where you save it. The next time you're faced with mental accounting, forget the %. Look at the $. You don't spend %. You spend $.

Well, back to refinancing. If you refinance an amount of money and get lower payments, you have to pay over a longer period of time. It's a no-brainer. While you've got your eight-year old car now refinanced for 15 years, consider that you'll soon have to have another car. Add up the numbers. You're probably paying more for total bills now than before refinancing. Refinance the house, but not the car, the washing machine or other miscellaneous items.

Even If you refinance just your home, and not at a lower interest rate to simply stretch out the years of payments, you're betting your home you can now become even more responsible than before and keep your head out of water. You can't borrow your way out of debt. You must "pay" your way out of debt. Paying your way out involves some soul-searching to see what you can do without, what you can do better and change the mental accounting process you failed to learn.

So, buckle down. Write down your total payments due by month for the next three years for each bill or expense. Then, start cutting out expenses you can do without. You'll now see your goal, to systematically pay down those bills until they're gone or manageable.

The next time someone says they'll give you something for nothing, just say, "Yeah, right" and walk away.

KEEP AN EYE ON YOUR 401K.

I know most of you are scared to death of trading stock and looking up all those numbers and trends necessary to keep pushing your investments ahead.

Let's face it. If you contribute to a 401k program at work, you can't just put your money in the hands of others and forget about it, expecting it to grow for you. You must carefully track your investments.

There are several warning signs that your 401k may be in trouble. Don't take for granted that the people hired by your company to handle your investment account are doing everything right. After all, this is your retirement money we're talking about.

You have to know how much you can contribute, what matching money the company will put into the plan, and which investment options are best for you. Depending on your age, your years left to work, and your comfort level; you have a lot of work ahead of you.

The money must be invested in your best interest. Investments must be diversified. You don't want to put all your eggs in one basket and then have the bottom fall out and lose all of them. If expenses exist for the plan, they must be reasonable. Your money must be invested carefully and wisely.

Rules aren't always followed. There are those who would divert your money to their own benefit and cause you to lose your retirement money. There are some warning signs you must watch to be sure your investment is safe and is handled correctly.

Your statement should come on a regular schedule. If it comes late consistently or comes at intervals that are irregular, beware. You should be getting quarterly statements if you are making contributions to the plan. If you aren't getting statements quarterly, you need to investigate. Call the plan administrator.

Check statements to be sure the employer contributions are credited to you. If not, contact the plan administrator and ask that this be corrected immediately.

If your statement balances are down and don't coincide with the market ups or downs, look into this immediately. I keep graphs and charts weekly to track my investments. Know the stock symbols for your investments and look them up at least once or twice a week.

Your company has strict rules about sending your contribution to the plan on a timely schedule. If your statement doesn't show your contribution amount, check into this.

If you doubt your contribution was credited to your account, look at your check stub and make sure the deduction is actually being made from your pay. Your payroll or human resources department should be able to help here.

If you hear that employees who have retired or left the company are not getting their benefit checks, look into this. If you roll over your retirement benefits to an IRA, make sure the company has sent the money to the IRA custodian.

Be sure of the investments you have authorized the plan to invest in for your. If your statement doesn't look like the ones you chose, look into this immediately. Your plan administrator may be investing aggressively to try to make up for high expenses, etc.

You may want to go to the trouble of seeing if the company investment managers or consultants are changed frequently. This could mean your company has something to hide.

If your company is in financial trouble, keep an eye on your investment program. It would be very tempting for the company to delay your contributions to the fund to use it in their interest instead of yours.

If you are computer literate, use the Excel program to track your investments. Set up a file to record the daily or weekly values of the investments you're into. Show a trend of the stock values. Record your account balance as often as possible. You should be able to use a pin number to open the web site your company has set up for the employees.

Be careful and don't expect everything to be done correctly. Most companies do a great job of administering the plans. There may be some that would quickly use your money to their advantage. Everyone is not honest. Just use common sense and be careful.

WHAT WERE POORHOUSES?

Poorhouses were tax-supported residential institutions to which people were required to go if they could not support themselves. They were started as a method of providing a less expensive (to the taxpayers) alternative to what we now call "welfare"—what was called "outdoor relief" in those days. People requested help from the community Over-seer of the Poor (sometimes called a Poor Master)—an elected town official. If the need was great or likely to be long-term, they were sent to the poorhouse instead of being given relief while they continued to live independently. Sometimes they were sent there even if they had not requested help from the Overseer of the Poor. Most of the time, that was usually done when they were found guilty of begging in public.

One misconception should be cleared up. They were not technically "debtors' prisons." Someone could owe a great deal on money, but if they could still provide them-selves the necessities for remaining independent they might avoid the poorhouse.

Prior to the establishment of poorhouses the problem of what to do with paupers in a community was dealt with in one of three ways:
Outdoor relief provided through an Overseer of the Poor: When people fall upon hard times and members of their family, friends or members of their church congregations could not provide enough assistance to tide them over, they made application to a local official called the Overseer of the Poor. Within a budget of tax money, he might provide them with food, fuel, clothing or even permission to get medical treatment to be paid out of tax funds.

Auctioning off the poor: People who could not support themselves (and their families) were put up for bid at a public auction. In an unusual type of auction, the pauper was sold to the bidder who would agree to provide room and board for the lowest price—usually this was for a specific period of a year or so. The person who got the contract got the use of the labor of the pauper and his/her family. This was actually a form of indent-ured servitude. It sounds a lot like slavery—except that it was technically not for the pauper's lifetime. And it had many of the perils of slavery. The welfare of the paupers depended almost entirely upon the kindness and fairness of the bidder. If he was to be motivated only by desire to make the minimum profit off the "use" of the pauper then concern for the bottom line might result in the pauper being denied adequate food, or safe and comfortable shelter, or even necessary medical treatment. And there often was very little recourse for protection against abuse.

Contracting with someone in the community to care for paupers: In this situation the care of the paupers was deligated to the person(s) who would contract to provide care at the lowest price. This system allowed the opportunity for somewhat better supervision as indicated in the terms of the contract—which might specify what minimum standard of care must be provided and that community officers would do inspections, etc. There were still often the same opportunities for abuses that were noted above.

Note: In some cases (before state laws began to require the establishment of County Poorhouses) local communities had already discovered that a place to house paupers helped reduce the cost of relief. These small town poorhouses were the prototypes for the later state-required county poorhouses. Those earlier poorhouses often instituted the use of an adjacent farm on which the paupers could work to raise their own food, thus making the house more self-sufficient (relying less on local tax funds). That is how the term "poor farm" came into being.

CELEBRITIES IN THE POORHOUSE

The story "Helen and Teacher" about Helen Keller and Anne Sullivan Macy, author Joseph P. Lash traces Anne Sullivan's early years in a Massachusetts poorhouse. The story describes her meeting with Helen Keller in Alabama, and goes on to account the joint events of their lives: Helen's childhood experiences, education at Radcliffe, and work in vaudeville, politics, and for the blind. This definitive biography concludes with Helen's final years without Anne Sullivan Macy.

Calamity Jane, who is well known all over the west, was taken violently ill on Friday last while on the train en route from Livingston to White Suplhur Springs. The auth-orities were notified by Agent Hoyt, and met her at the depot. She was out of funds and consequently taken to the Poor Farm, where under the treatment of county physician Safley and careful nursing of Mr. Holmes, she was discharged on Monday and went on her way rejoicing. She still has for sale copies of her picture and the little pamphlet pur-porting to be a history of her life.

Annie Oakley was born on August 13, 1860 in Darke County, Ohio. The fifth daughter of Jacob and Susan Moses, the Quaker family had migrated to Ohio after the family tavern in Hollidaysburg, Pennsylvania burned. Jacob Moses died of pneumonia in 1866. for the next several years, Annie helped her family by trapping and performing chores on the family farm.

At the age of eight or nine, she went to live with the Superintendent's family at the county farm. At one point during her stay at the poor farm, she was "lent out" to a local farm family as a servant. According to her autobiography, this family abused her mentally and physically. After two years, she ran back to the poor farm and remained there until she was thirteen or fourteen. While there, she learned to sew and received an education.

OVER THE HILL TO THE POOR-HOUSE

BY: WILL CARLETON, 1897

Over the hill to the poor-house I'm trudgin' my weary way—
I, a woman of seventy, and only a trifle gray—
I, who am smart an' chipper, for all the years I've told,
As many another woman that's only half as old.

Over the hill to the poor-house—I can't quite make it clear!
Over the hill to the poor-house—it seems so horrid queer!
Many a step I've taken, a-toilin' to and fro,
But this is a sort of journey I never thought to go.

What is the use of heapin' on me a pauper's shame?
Am I lazy or crazy? Am I blind or lame?
True, I am not so supple, nor yet so awful stout;
But charity ain't no favor, if one can live without.

I am ready and winnin' an' anxious any day
To work for a decent livin' and pay my honest way;
For I can earn my victuals, an' more, too, I'll be bound,
If anyone is winnin' to only have me 'round.

Once I was young an' handsome—I was, upon my soul—
Once my cheeks was roses, my eyes was black as coal;
And I can't remember, in them days, of hearin' people say,
For any kind of a reason, that I was in their way!

Taint no use of boastin' or talkin' over-free,

But many a house an' home was open then to me;
Many a han'some offer I had from likely men,
And nobody ever hinted that I was a burden then.

And when to John I was mrried, sure he was good and smart,
But he and all the neighbors would own I done my part;
For life was all before me, an' was young an' strong,
And I worked by best an' smartest in tryin' to get along.

And so we worked together; and life was hard, but gay,
With now and then a baby to cheer us on our way.
Till we had half a dozen, an' all growed clean an' neat,
An' went to school like others, an' had enough to eat.

An' so we worked for the child'rn and raised 'em every one—
Worked for 'em summer and winter, just as we ought to've done;
Only perhaps we humored 'em, which some good folks condemn,
But every couple's own child'rn's a heap the dearest to them!

Strange how much we think of our blessed little ones!—
I'd have died for my daughters, and I's have died for my sons.
And God he made that rule of love; but when we're old and gray
I've noticed it sometimes, somehow, fails to work the other way.

Strange another thing: when our boys an' girls was grown,
And when, exceptin' Charley, they'd left us there alone,
When john he nearer an' nearer came, an' dearer seemed to be,
The Lord of hosts, he came one day an' took him away from me!

Still I was bound to struggle, an' never cringe or fall—
Still I worked for Charley, for Charley was now my all;
And Charley was pretty good to me, with scarce a word or frown,
Till at last he went a-courtin', and brought a wife from town.

She was somewhat dressy, an' hadn't a pleasant smile—
She was quite conceity, and carried a heap o' style;
But if ever I tried to be friends, I did with her, I know;
But she was hard and haughty, an' we couldn't make it go.

She had an edication, and that was good for her,
But when she twitted me on mine, "twas carrin' things too far,

225

An' I told her once, 'fore company, (an almost made her sick)
That I never had seen a mansion that was big enough for two.

An' I never could speak to suit her, never could please her eye,
An' it made me independent, an' then I didn't try.
But I was terribly humbled, an' felt it like a blow,
When Charley turned agin me, an' told me I could go.

I went to live with Susan, but Susan's house was small,
And she was always a-hintin' how snug it was for us all;
And that with her husband's sisters, and what with childr'rn three,
Twas easy to discover there wasn't room for me.

An' then I went with Thomas, the oldest son I've got:
For Thomas's buildings'd cover the half of an acre lot,
But all the child'rn was on me—I couldn't stand their sauce—
And Thomas said I needn't think I was comin' thereto boss.

An' then I wrote to Rebecca, my girl who lives out west,
And to Isaac, not far from her—some twenty miles at best;
And one of 'em said 'twas too warm there for anyone so old,
And t'other had an opinion the climate was too cold.

So they have shirded and slighted me, an' shifted me about—
So they have well nigh soured me, an' wore my old heart out;
But still I've borne up pretty well, an' wasn't much put down,
Till Charley went to the poor-master, an' put me on the town!

Over the hill to the poor-house—my child'rn dear, good-bye!
Many a night I've watched you when only God was nigh;
And God'll judge between us; but I will al'ays pray
That you shall never suffer the half that I do to-day!

POORHOUSES THEN

In 1843 a Government Commission on Poor Relief in Scotland reported that the general standard of care was low. Unemployed man, deserted women, orphaned children, unmarried mothers, the aged, the mentally or physically handicapped and the rural victims of crop failures all found themselves in need of aid. In many cases the existing system was unable to cope. At that time there were only 13 poorhouses in Scot-land, but in 1863 there were 48, with 16 more under construction.

The poorhouse had to tread the delicate line between offering a refuge for the genuinely needy and ensuring that those who were capable of earning a living felt no inclination to stay longer than necessary. The poorhouse population was constantly changing with inmates frequently admitted at the time of crises and then re-admitted when problems beset them again.

The poorhouse aimed to educate children to earn their living, but in many cases this education was inadequate. In one poorhouse, 35 under-fives were kept in a nursery with no toys of any kind. In another, a so-called "school master" was engaged merely to keep the children quiet and punish them if they stepped out of line.

Adults were put to work if able. Men helped with the maintenance of the building and, as far as possible, followed their own trades. Women worked in the laundry, clean-ed, cooked and sewed. Even the elderly were not exempt, with old men carrying fire-wood, and old women were expected to knit. Barnhill Poorhouse in Springburn covered the whole of the north part of Glasgow and, in the early part of this century there were 2,000 inmates with members of staff.

On admission, people were assessed according to their condition and abilities and any who required treatment were referred to hospitals. Efforts were made to have children boarded out with neighboring families. This had the additional advantage of freeing their mothers to find employment and so leave the poorhouse.

Inmates were required to wear the poorhouse clothing to discourage any attempts to escape. The clothing was of relatively good quality, and some people sought admission to kit themselves out. Then they disappeared with the clothes.

Vagrants sometimes came in to have their verminous clothing treated in the poorhouse delousing machine.

There was usually enough food, but sometimes it lacked nutritional value. Breakfast might have been porrige, and lunch broth, with potatoes and sometimes cheese. In many poorhouses, tea was a luxury reserved for the elderly.

The end of the poorhouse system came in sight in 1928 when Neville Chamberlain, then the Minister of Health, passed a Bill to repeal the Poor Law Amendment Act which had made the poorhouse the only legal source of relief.

On March 31, 1930 the poorhouse ceased to exist, although they remained in all but name for some years after. It was not until 1948 that the National Insurance Act, Nation-al Health Service Act and National Assistance Act sought to remove the place of the poorhouse in society. Barn-hill Poorhouse became Forrest-Hall Hospital until its demo-lition in the 1980's.

POORHOUSES NOW

As you've already read now, you know the circumstances under which someone would be qualified for or actually put into a poorhouse. A lot of the circumstances are still around today. We certainly won't call any of the three examples I'm going to give you as poorhouses. Let's now look at some examples of situations in which people find themselves and see if you think they're somewhat related to the poorhouse era.

We certainly see unemployed men, deserted women, orphaned children, unmarried mothers, the aged, physically and mentally handicapped, etc. All these people find them-selves in need of the same things that people in 1830 needed. We also see the delicate line between offering a refuge for the genuinely needy and ensuring that those who want to take advantage of the system and live off it.

One example of a modern-day poorhouse is the mortgaged home of a family of four, two workers, two children, a dog or cat, two cars (probably suv's) and up to their eye-balls in debt with no hope of getting any better. In some cases, this scenario is worse than that of poorhouse days. People are deeper in debt than then, can't see any way out of their situation and can't afford their lifestyle. These people are residing in their own poorhouse, not looked after by a Superintendent or others in charge. They're on their own to wrestle every day to get a little closer to breaking even. Little do they know or think of how they got there in the first place. They have definitely "spent their way to the poorhouse."

Today, there are many "rest homes" in which elderly and not-so-elderly men and women have either been placed by relatives or have no choice but to go there to be taken care of and given day-to-day needs. They are fed, clothed, given medical help and are virtually dependent upon those in charge. This sounds very much like the old days of the poorhouses, doesn't it? The biggest difference is that people in these places have very little to say about their lives and are not required to work in any way to help pay for their stays. Most are there because their families either can't look after them or are too busy trying to avoid going there themselves to take care of them.

The current government instituted "welfare" system has in itself taken away the chance for individuals to exhort their own capabilities to work and care for themselves. Instead, the government pays for housing, issues food stamps and subsidizes other things for them. This Is not the way to let Americans become the best they can be by working and helping themselves and their families. Some surely need help to get them out of a bad situation, but then the God-given ability to work and support your family should be put into action. Such people are trapped in a never-ending revolving door in which they can't escape and have no desire to remove themselves from. With work programs and social services help, this segment of America could overcome their problems and use their abilities to better themselves and thereby break the revolving door syndrome. These comments are not to disgrace or show unconcern, but to help them escape from the poor-house environment and live a better life.

So, you can see that the idea of a poorhouse hasn't changed that much. We now see such people in every walk of life, not in a large white house on the hill, looked after by others, but struggling to overcome the vast enticements to draw them into financial ruin. We must overcome this mentality and take control of our lives, thus training our children to do the same, thereby creating a country of people who think for themselves and know how to survive well, not survive only.

I hope this book will open your eyes to the problems that bombard you every day. I also hope it encourages you to take financial charge of your lives and allows you to have a better and happier future.

TO SUM IT UP

Okay, we've discussed everything from curbing spending to investment strategy. Let's look at the sum of what we've learned or chosen to ignore in this book.

You must have or have had a credit or financial problem, or you wouldn't have bought my book. Something had to drive you to accepting the fact that you either needed help or just wanted to see what the book was all about. Maybe you were just curious about how to avoid the poorhouse.

Some of you may be kicking yourself for reading such a book because you now must face your financial problems head on and do something about them. Others may still be in denial of your money problems and have no intention of making a change. If you've gotten this far, you surely have read something you badly needed to be shown or to know.

It's true that the original poorhouses are gone now, but you may still be living in one or are destined to do so because of your reckless financial decisions. Those who resided in the poorhouses in the early 1800's may have been better off than some of you today. They got fed and taken care of. They didn't have 30-year mortgages to pay off. They didn't have a $500 monthly car payment. They didn't even have a home or a car. They were at the bottom of their financial pit they had fallen into. And they were probably better money managers than a lot of people today.

Have you made a conscious effort to change the way you spend money? I hope you have. Have you decided to start saving for a rainy day? Have you learned what money really is?

A lot of you have been in denial for years about how you spend. If you've got money left over, you buy or do something with it. If not, you simply charge it and hope you can pay it a little at a time on credit cards.

To sincerely make a change, you must admit your irresponsibility with handling money, saving money and building a nest egg. You must change something, and this begins with a family meeting or meetings to discuss expenses and income. If you are not making a profit, you are letting your family down.

If you're still at the point where you say you're getting by, but not saving, remember that unexpected expenses can ruin a budget and create havoc in the family. You must admit to yourself that things happen that will strain your budget. You do have a budget, don't you?

I sincerely want to ask you to get your family together and go over the things you've read and learned in the book. With input from all members of the family, you can actually climb up out of the hole you're in.

If you're a frugal person who pays his/her bills on time and saves some of their earnings, maybe you've picked up a tip or two that will help you achieve your goals.

It's never too late to start saving and planning for the future. It doesn't matter if you're 20,30,40,50 or 60, the future is still in front of you. You may just have less time to react and plan for it.

Please don't just throw this book into the shelf or drawer somewhere and forget about it. You may want to go back to parts of it for help or just read it all again to get the most from it. I really believe there is a great need today for people to realize where they are financially and learn how to avoid a disaster or be ready for one when it comes.

If you think this book has helped you and you have a friend or family member who may enjoy reading it, loan them your book or let them know where they can get one. We're all in the same boat together, even though some of us don't have a paddle.

You may still want to attend a money management class. They're all over and shouldn't be hard to find. Learn all you can and pass it on to your kids, family members and friends. We all need all the help possible to fight the urges to spend, spend and spend.

Make a dedicated commitment to yourself and your family to start today, not to-morrow, to take control of your financial destiny. It's your battle to fight, and it is a battle in today's world. You have a responsibility to your children to see that they learn to spend and save correctly. Who knows? This may even mean they won't depend on you for money when they are grown.

Thanks for letting me share some ideas and secrets with you. I sincerely hope they will help your immensely.

About the Author

The author has spent most of his life handling financial problems in his career as Cost Accountant, Industrial Engineer and Plant Manager. He is very qualified to write this book, and it is his sincere desire that you will learn from the book how to avoid financial pitfalls and how to get out of them if you need to.

With financial control getting harder and harder these days, you need to know the tools necessary to get you on the road to financial success, not by necessarily investing in stocks, but by operating your home finances in such a was as to become wealthier and happier while doing it. This book will teach you this.